Protect Yourself:
The Simple Keys Women Need to be Safe and Secure

Doris

Always be safe!

Thanks

Protect Yourself:
The Simple Keys Women Need to be Safe and Secure

Steve A. Kovacs

iUniverse, Inc.
New York Lincoln Shanghai

Protect Yourself:
The Simple Keys Women Need to be Safe and Secure

iUniverse books may be ordered through booksellers or by contacting:

iUniverse
2021 Pine Lake Road, Suite 100
Lincoln, NE 68512
www.iuniverse.com
1-800-Authors (1-800-288-4677)

These pages are written as a community service for those interested in the subjects of women's safety and security. The reader understands that the author is not a lawyer, nor engaged in the practice of law, and is not rendering legal advice. The author shall have no liability to any persons or entities with respect to any loss, liability or damage alleged to be caused by the application of information or opinions published in this book.

ISBN-13: 978-0-595-38208-8 (pbk)
ISBN-13: 978-0-595-82577-6 (ebk)
ISBN-10: 0-595-38208-8 (pbk)
ISBN-10: 0-595-82577-X (ebk)

Printed in the United States of America

This book is dedicated to Dak who always was ready to protect and love, a great combination.

Contents

Introduction xi

CHAPTER 1   What Criminals Look For, and how knowing it can
cut your chances of assault by over 50%. 1

CHAPTER 2   Home Security 5

CHAPTER 3   Being Safe While On the Go 22

CHAPTER 4   THE WORKPLACE, the surprising area of danger
and how to deal with it 42

CHAPTER 5   Dating and Socializing. 46

CHAPTER 6   Rape and Sexual Assault 52

CHAPTER 7   Tools To Protect Women, all the way from
toasters to handguns, it's your choice. 59

CHAPTER 8   Self-Defense When Being Attacked 72

CHAPTER 9   Defending Yourself in an Attack 81

CHAPTER 10   BEING RAPED, THE AFTERMATH, and how
you can survive and flourish. 96

CHAPTER 11   Custom Made for Your Needs, the way YOU
choose what you need to be safe 99

About the Author 101

Acknowledgements

I thankfully acknowledge the people who were instrumental in helping with this book. From Paula Mangino, Michael Garrett, Elizabeth Zak, Mary Dinardo and Jeff Balasz whom all were instrumental in its completion. And importantly, I acknowledge all the victims I have come in contact with who motivated me to spring forward and write this book of help, faith and knowledge.

Introduction

This book was written for all women that have the potential to become a victim of crime. In reality, this of course means all women. It's for the young and old who can be harmed and feel that distressing fear, women can and quite often, do feel. Also, this book is for the women who have been victims, who feel that they have been made vulnerable and cold in this world. It's for those who feel that life will never be the same for them because of what they have experienced. It is for those women who feel all alone, different and possibly, deeply isolated because of what they have experienced. It's written partially in the hope of instilling into women victims of crime, and also to those who have not been victims, that some people actually *do care and are on their side.* Besides for what and for whom it is written, most importantly, that there are strategies to help all women.

To the women who have been victims, you will never be the same. None of us really stay the same. You have been touched by something bad and it will always be with you. That does not mean that it will be with you only in a negative way. You can turn that nightmare into a new realistic viewpoint of life, of your self, and realize that there is peace and comfort for you in the world, no matter what has happened to you. In reality, I mean no matter what has happened to you! Yes, you can gain from your victimization and have peace. It's a matter of perspective. Get the positive perspective of acceptance, understanding, knowledge and strength.

This book contains common sense solutions and strategies to make a woman's life safer. *There are simple basic cornerstone keys that can make you safe and secure and even save your life.* It is put together using my personal years of experience, training and observation. I have seen what works and what is, let's call it, flight of the imagination self-defense, or in other words unrealistic, more-harm-than good self-defense guidance. There will be little spinning of "truths" in this book. It's geared toward reality and not fluff. I think it was James Brown the "*Godfather of Soul*" who sang the words: "Reality doesn't lie." This book is about reality.

If you do not want to be a victim of crime, there are certain things that work, things that you can do. There are certain basic behaviors and precautions that all of us can do.

There are no guaranties that you will not be a victim of crime. You can do everything right and still become a victim. It also doesn't mean that you are at fault or less of a woman if you become one. However, again there are things you can do to lessen the *chance* that you will be a *VICTIM*. I'm not suggesting that you use every single suggestion discussed in the book for your safety and security. To use every single tip all the time would be unrealistic and not expected. Pick and choose the strategies that may be more appropriate for your personal lifestyle.

Toward the end of 1999 the federal government came out with its yearly nationwide crime statistics. Basically their statistics, which they gather from reporting police departments from across the United States, stated that crime had gone down for another year. This downward trend had been going on for a number of years. Violent crime as well as property crime was reported down. Generally speaking, these crimes went down in the area of ten percent.

There are a number of reasons experts feel crime rates have been dropping for a number of years. A decent economy, more police, better policing, the decline of teenagers or younger adults in our country presently, and other miscellaneous facts are the reasons for the consistent drop. One of these reasons mentioned most often, the lesser amount of teenagers or younger adults in our society, has been a generally agreed upon reason, with many experts as a major explanation, why crime statistically is down.

Younger people commit most crime and for a number of years our country's population has been low in this regard. However, experts say we will have a steady increase of teenagers in our country in the early 2000s. As of 2003 most crime statistics continued their downward turn and in some cases down to their lowest rates in thirty years.

Everything Isn't Rosy

The day after I read the crime statistics for 1999 I was eating breakfast and reading the newspaper. I read that the city of Detroit was on alert after a number of youngsters were raped since the beginning of their school year. Eight girls had been raped and twenty-six girls also reported attempts to abduct them. The rapes occurred when the girls were on the way to or coming from school. I then turned the page of my local newspaper and read that at the University of Massachusetts female students were gathering at the college. They were chanting anti-violence slogans and carrying signs saying: *Protect Our Women* and *Too Little, Too Late*. In less than a month's time four women had been assaulted at the University and the women felt that not enough was being done to help them with their safety.

The fact is that crime has been going down for years and 1999 was yet another year with a downward spiral. Excellent news but you wouldn't want to tell the girls in Detroit, or the young women at the University of Massachusetts and the countless others who continue to be victims of crime, that crime is down and things are looking just rosy.

A month or so after I read that 2003 was yet another banner year for the continuing downward crime trend, I read that one local city was having an alarming increase in murders and a high number of rapes. Crimes continue against women and in many areas at a high level. Changes may occur in our country and crime statistics may go up. Economies change, morals change, age trends go up and down, and accepted norms come and go. *Crime is here to stay.* It will get better and it will get worse. Until a solid core change takes place and holds true and strong for humanity, crime will be waiting around the corner. Let's just keep that in our minds, not freak out about it but be aware. Rapes and sexual assaults occur and women need to do all they can to be safe and continue their lives pursuing their passions and goals.

So remember, *unfortunately* crime is here to stay. *However,* better policing, better awareness on your part and better direction and training of our children, will all help the good statistics rise in our favor. By reading this book you are actually doing your part for a common good.

Been There Done That

I have been a working police officer in a supervisory role and have been involved in both public law enforcement and private sector security management for more than twenty years. Not only have I seen a lot of things, but also and just as importantly, I have a law enforcement and self-defense mindset. Many of my friends and relatives have been involved in law enforcement. I've talked to other law enforcement men and women from other agencies from around the country and have discussed crime trends and situations with various experts. I have also been involved in Martial Arts for literally most of my life, from about the age of eight. My family and I have taught thousands of students self-defense for years. I have seen many different instructors and self-defense students throughout these years and I have seen what is realistic and what I feel is not workable or useable. *Most importantly*, I have also been a victim of crime.

Once as a young child I was probably a minute or so away from death. While playing with a close friend in a wooded park behind my house, a neighborhood teenager who apparently had mental problems, approached my friend and me. This boy who was about fifteen or sixteen years-old, was involved in some bizarre behavior in the neighborhood, including setting the woods on fire a couple of times.

My friend and I were about five or six years old, very innocent, and easy prey for a predator. The guy saw us playing in the woods and came up to us. He talked to us for a short time, about what I really can't recall. Nevertheless, what I do remember is that he said he was going to hang me. Yes, hang me! Well, he did just what he said he was going to do and wrapped a belt around my neck, tossed the belt over a tree branch and started to hang me.

I don't remember if I fought or not. I don't think I did. I do remember that I screamed for my older brother, Frank, about six or seven times. I also remember, vividly, that I thought that I would only be able to call for help one more time. I was passing out. I knew that I was on the verge of unconsciousness. I knew inside of me that it was the end and I was going to die. In retrospect, it's pretty amazing a child of that age can rationally understand that physically they only have a few seconds left. I also vividly remember hearing tree branches breaking as if a buffalo was raging through the woods. The buffalo was my brother who was six years older than I was and had heard, as he later told me, my blood-curdling screams. When he saw my brother, the predator let me go and started running away.

Frank untied my neck and quickly looked to see if I was "OKAY." He then chased the teenager who had a huge head start on him. Frank was athletic, physically fit and good at fighting. He also was a fast runner. Frank chased him for about half a mile and caught him on his front doorstep, where he administered his own type of justice.

My brother and I both believe that I probably would have lost my life if someone hadn't intervened when he did…especially when he saw how badly I was injured as he released the noose from around my neck. In this case I was totally vulnerable, an innocent child with no physical way to protect myself.

My heart goes out to all the vulnerable children who did not have a big brother there when they were accosted or killed.

My heart goes out to all the vulnerable women who did not have someone there to protect them in their time of need. My heart going out is nice and I believe important but it's not enough. *Strategies, experience and any knowledge I can convey to help you, are more important.*

This book can give suggestions that help women to help themselves to the point where they do not become a victim. I'm convinced that someone will read something in this book and it will help her not to be a victim. If you follow certain behaviors and take certain precautions we can lower the percentage of victims. If women follow some of the tips in the book it unquestionably can and likely will help someone.

After my hanging incident, when I was about eleven-years old I was again an attempted victim of crime, a robbery. The difference for me when I was eleven was that I took an active role in not dying, in not being hurt, in not being abused. Most importantly, it worked for me. It can also work for you. I'll talk about that incident later in the book.

Women have been targets of crimes since the dawn of time. Children and men have been and are targets also, but women have been and still are, in a different class of crimes committed against them. For generations they were considered second-class citizens and in some cultures still are. Women have been treated as a piece of property to be dealt with as such, to not being given the right to vote, and to being sexually violated and domestically abused. They have been grabbed by the "stronger sex," robbed, assaulted and generally used for what they can provide, without much thought of the feelings and damage inflicted on them.

Times and conditions have changed for women and are improving constantly and thankfully, consistently. However, women still have their own specific concerns and problems to deal with. This book addresses many of these concerns and gives the reader workable common sense advice and strategies. So let's start and see what is appropriate for your unique needs and desires.

Innocence Lost

While patrolling as a policeman one warm summer evening, I talked to the mother of a seventeen year-old girl who had come home from work the night before, crying. She told her mom that, after getting off of work at a family restaurant at about 10 p.m., she pulled into a gas station to fill up her gas-tank. The restaurant was in a good neighborhood, as was the gas station. The station, however, was frequented by a bad element. The girl was gassing her car up at the pumps when a group of men started talking to her. They too were pumping gas and were friendly and respectful at first.

The daughter was an enthusiastic, trusting, friendly, pretty, young woman. She went on and talked to the men who looked a little concerning to her as she later recounted, but they were polite and she was polite back. They then started talking aggressively about sex. They started "hitting" on her in an aggressive way, not caring about her feelings. They became more aggressive and she became frightened and did not know what to do. Thankfully, there were other people at the station and nothing further happened to her, other than verbal abuse. The girl was shocked and frightened, from what she thought was going to be an innocent conversation that she expected to be just an exchange of simple pleasantries, turning into essentially an act of harassment and abuse.

I generally did not let emotion effect me in my line of work, but hearing about this relatively minor incident made me a little sad. The incident is really no big deal; nobody got hurt, raped or killed. However, what it told me was that it was a core issue that women have to go through sometimes.

In reality every woman should go through what the incident *showed* the young girl. Every woman should see life realistically, the good, the bad and the ugly. Parents and others owe it to young women to help them see what life is like sometimes, and offer them knowledge to cope, understand and thrive.

What happened here was that a nice young woman was being friendly, polite and enthusiastic, in talking with her fellow human beings. She said they looked a little scary but she didn't let that deter her. She was going to be friendly and nice anyway. What she got that night was a dose of a sad reality that women have to deal with at times. It was sad to think of a young person trying to be friendly and nice getting mistreated in the fashion that she was. Innocence lost.

All was not lost for her, though. What happened to her doesn't necessarily mean that she has to turn into a mean, sour-faced, unfriendly, anxious or paranoid person. Similar incidents like this one start many people on the road to bitterness.

Now, what is this girl likely to do the next time a man, or possibly several men start up a conversation or compliment her? She may just be aloof and not answer back. She may get a mean looking scowl on her face and walk away. Possibly, she may actually retort back with a mean comment. I'm not going to say whether I think either of these actions would be the right or wrong things for her to do, because we will actually focus on *your personal abilities to discern the correct actions for you, at the correct time.* It is not for any one to tell you exactly what is right and wrong for you during a personal confrontational incident, you are the one that can, must and will decide that. What I am saying though, is that these types of incidents are reality, a certain reality most women, sadly, learn to deal with, sometimes at a very early age. *It is a primer in the uniqueness* of the problems women deal with.

Just as with this incident, other incidents where women become actual crime victims or in their attempts not to be a victim still does not mean that they have to become mean, bitter or hidden away in fear. On the contrary, you will learn that you can deal with whatever comes your way, and still be yourself. You *can adapt* to particular circumstances and yes…be mean, strong and aggressive *during the incident* and yet be a fun loving, normal woman before and after the episode. Predators should not be able to cloud your positive development.

Our concerns will focus on how to stay safe from sexual assault, rape and any other areas of physical abuse women can be confronted with.

For me, the incident at the gas station showed me the foundation of the unique "things" women have to deal with, confronting predatory people. It opened my eyes to your unique plight and helped to motivate me in helping women.

Your issues are distinctive; they can start off relatively innocuous as it did for this young woman and can go up levels in intensity, from groping to sexual assault or to rape. These things all can happen to women and *importantly women can deal with all of them!*

With the proper direction and strategies the girl in this incident just like you, no matter what you may face someday, or possibly have faced, can still maintain her or your "nice-ness." Furthermore, I think that is the key, to be able to survive and get by in our world and yet keep and develop our unique humanity. It's about facing life enthusiastically with a positive, friendly yet realistic outlook. You deserve it and importantly, you can attain it.

Lessening the Odds

There are things we can all do to lessen the odds of becoming a victim. In the pages to follow are some of the things we can do to keep from being an easy mark for a predator.

1

What Criminals Look For, and how knowing it can cut your chances of assault by over 50%.

Before we get into the things you can do to safeguard you and your home, I want to go over what kind of people commit crimes. I am not a criminologist or sociologist and I do not want to get into to all the specific social situations that may cause people to commit crimes. I will, however, talk about the street reality of the average criminal. Who the bad guys are and why and what kind of targets they look for.

Muggers, thieves, burglars and criminals in general look for the *easy way to get what they want*. We all like the easier way, but the bad guys take this mantra to the highest degree. This is a fact. They are predators who generally prey on the weak. Let me repeat this, *they generally prey on the weak*.

They are similar to the predatory animal in the jungle. The lion, leopard or tiger look for the weakest, slowest, easiest target to pounce on. If there is an injured animal in a herd, the predatory animal will go for the weak or injured. If there is a newborn animal in the herd, they will pounce on it. If they see a preoccupied animal, or one that is sleeping or vulnerable, they will go for him or her. They do not look for the most prepared, strongest and fastest animal in the jungle. Criminals are the same; they look for the easiest target. It may be the easiest home to break into or the easiest "looking" person walking down the street to attack. This is a simple truth that can give you an upper hand in not becoming a victim of crime. It's a cornerstone in gaining knowledge about personal safety. This knowledge will give you a mindset that can steer you in the right direction, the direction needed to not be a victim. Some may say, of course bad guys go for the weakest target, that's so basic, that's nothing new. Yes it is, but in the hustle and bustle of life many women do not remember this basic fact or realize what it really means.

It means being *aware* of this basic foundational fact and working to make it *less* in your disfavor. Knowing it because someone tells you so and just putting it in the back of your mind is not the way to handle it. *You must feel it and know it deep down inside and all of your daily tasks will go more in your favor, safety and security wise.*

Critical! How to Present Yourself

Appearances are quite important at times. The way we look and come across can be a significant factor in our safety and security.

The Way You Look

When I talked about criminals going after the easy, weakest target it is essential for you to keep in mind that if you appear to them to be slow, weak or submissive, you may have a problem. You very well may appear to them as *that* easy target. However, if you walk with your head up and with an air of confidence, with a look and physical bearing that exudes "If you mess with me you're really going to have your work cut out for you," you *certainly* lessen your chance of being that victim.

As an example, imagine two women walking down a street. They both weigh the same and are the same age. They both are dressed similarly with the same type of jewelry on. They are walking on opposite sides of the street. In the shadows, there is a predator, and he needs money to feed his drug habit. He's just about dying to get another fix. He can hardly wait to get some money. Soon, he'll get drugged up and he thinks he'll feel free. He can hardly wait. He, however, needs money now. One woman coming towards him has her head down; her shoulders slumped a little, and is walking timidly and slowly.

The other woman has her head high up, her chest out and shoulders straight. She is walking at a fast, strong pace. The look on her face shows strength, confidence and purpose.

She looks around as she walks using crisp, aware, together glances. The look of *purpose* shows that she is going somewhere and nothing is apt to stop her from getting there or fulfilling her purpose. The predator thinks…the one who is slow and pliable looks doable. He thinks the other one looks stronger, but hey, she's only a woman. I can take her, too. He thinks again, the timid and weak looking one is surely going to *give him less of a hassle.* Common sense tells him that. "I'll go for her. She shouldn't give me much of a problem." He makes his move and goes for the weaker appearing one.

I think if you give it some thought you'd agree with me. In plain English he is most likely going to go after the easiest appearing target. *He does not want a hard time.* A woman who is strong, determined and purposeful will give him *that hard time.* Strength, determination and sense of purpose are strong forces for anyone. Don't look easier! *Look confident, vibrant and alive. Look like you will be, at the bare minimum, a big hassle.*

Must we be Mean, Cold and Harsh?

We can walk with confidence without coming across like a nut or mean person. If you must make eye contact, make it short and strong. Walk as though you are not going to be victimized. As though, if someone messes with you, you will be a handful or even a nightmare for them. As if though you will scream, bite, kick and poke. In short be *assertive*, not passive or aggressive.

You can learn this type of general bearing when needed and yet not appear to be a wild woman out of a jungle. Look and feel as though you are not and will not be a victim. Like "don't even think about it buddy, I'm not the one. If you choose me you're going to open up a can of problems for yourself and you *don't* want problems."

You can turn this on and off, so to speak. When you're walking and feel the need to be ready for protection, you can up the level of your general bearing and attitude. Years ago when I was teaching children's self-defense classes, I was talking to a mother of a student near the mat where the class was being conducted. We were seated, having a nice, peaceful, friendly talk, I really can't remember about what, but I do remember it was a mellow conversation.

Well, I was called up to spar with another instructor as was customary towards the end of the classes. I excused myself to the woman, who happened to be the wife of a concert violinist with the world renowned Cleveland Philharmonic Orchestra, and went up and started fighting my opponent. As usual, for me, when I fought I was very aggressive, vocal and vicious in my fighting. The fight lasted a couple of minutes and after I finished I immediately sat down next to the woman and started continuing our conversation. In mid-conversation she stopped me and asked me how I "did that?" "Did what?" I asked. She said a few seconds ago you were screaming, (karate type grunting) vicious, and extremely aggressive and now you sit down, are calm, relaxed and you start talking as if you almost hadn't even left the conversation. I told her "a few seconds ago I was fighting, now I'm talking." She paused for a second or two, seemed to ponder a little, and started up where we left off.

I was not anything special and wasn't touched by some unusual martial art calmness or power. I was a person that through training, experience and searching, knew that *actions are different*. When you're talking pleasantly with someone that's what it is, *talking*, pleasantly. When you're fighting, you are *fighting*. Fighting means battle between two people, and battle is just that, nothing else, and battle consists of serious, bad intentioned action. Once the battle is over, it's over. It's simple. As an example, when you're engrossed in watching your favorite television drama and your 4 year old daughter looks at you lovingly and says "I love you," you lose sight of that intense drama for a few seconds, hug your daughter and tell her you love her back. Then in a heartbeat, you can get right back into the drama. Two separate actions can be divided into their respective places. This goes for self-defense too. You can turn up levels of your bearing or behavior, up and down, more or less. It's not being fake either, *it's adapting to your surroundings for that particular moment.*

Reducing the Odds of Being Chosen as a Victim

Knowing that criminals do not want difficult targets and that they look for the *easy way to get what they want*, whatever that "easy" may be at a particular time, gives you the upper hand. Yes, it gives you an upper hand simply by your understanding of it and then you striving to never appear to be *that* easy target. Also knowing that,

- Strength

- Determination

- Sense of Purpose

are actually strong forces in your arsenal of being less of a target for a predator. Have that purposeful attitude, have the bearing that shows you will not be a pushover. Like the attitude of I'm going somewhere or doing something and nothing's going to stop me.

Also knowing that you can turn this up and down as needed will help you to realize that a certain time may be the right time to turn the level of reaction up. These "keys" alone can give you a better than 50% chance of not being chosen to be a target. Couple this basic foundational safety "key" with some other concrete steps of safety and security and you're well on your way to a safer and securer family and self.

It's time to break down some specific security needs, discuss them and find the solutions for your safety.

2

Home Security

We all have homes, which are usually our comfort zones away from the hustle and bustle of the world. People have lived and felt like this for generations. Whether it is a one-bedroom apartment or a twenty-room house, our home shelters us from outside perils. Our home is our safe space. Years ago it was the caves that our ancestors lived in. Today they are the condominiums, apartments and houses that we call home.

Many of us have felt the nervousness of hearing unusual noises at night while nestled away in our homes. What was that noise? Is it something to worry about? Should we get up and see what it is?

Watching a scary movie and hearing a strange noise can trigger anxiety. Many people feel uncomfortable being alone at home at night and many wives feel uncomfortable when their husbands are out of town on business and they're left alone.

Late at night there may be no television or radio noise, little or no automobile traffic sounds, just silence. When there is silence, every little sound can be heard, such as the natural creaky sounds of a house that may be settling or reacting to the weather, to the sounds of the wind, or animals that may be near to—or actually on your home.

Know this, in the silence of the night these sounds are magnified and, although these sounds may be there during the day, at night without the masking noises of the day we notice them. These are all common concerns and fears that many people have. I have been on countless police calls of house noises at night that turned out to be benign.

When we hear stories of homes being burglarized, or worse yet, someone being assaulted or killed in their home, it really hits a chord for us. Being violated in THE SAFE SHELTER is shocking. People who have experienced burglaries often take it as a deep personal violation. They come home and find their homes ransacked and their personal items stolen. They are shaken to their core that their safe personal space has been violated. How could this happen? The place where they felt safe and secure was touched by an intruder who was able to come into their personal lives, their shelter. Can they ever feel safe again?

A terrible crime spree that illustrates this fear to me is the infamous California case of the Night Stalker. Someone was entering homes, assaulting and killing people, repeatedly. It seemed like the killing was not going to stop and the murderer was never going to be caught. Needless to say the community was terrified. As a matter of fact, I know a woman personally who lived in the area during the time of the murders and she tells me everyone was just about scared stiff, wondering if overnight they were going to be the next victims. Another example is Charles Manson and his blindly following gang who killed actress Sharon Tate inside of her home. Both of these situations were high profile invasions of homes where assaults, torture and murders occurred.

Assaults, rapes and countless burglaries occur every year in our nation's homes. *The good news though, is that the home is still a safe place for us, statistically.*

Burglary Statistics

The statistics below were compiled by the Burglary Prevention Council and can be enlightening to those of us interested in our own and our family's safety.

Every eleven seconds, burglars break into a house, apartment or condominium. Nationwide there are over two million burglaries a year. Sixty percent of these burglaries occur during the daylight hours.

The losses by victims are estimated at over three billion dollars. The average loss per burglary is $1,350.

July is the month that statistics say most burglaries occur. February had the least.

The South was the region with the highest volume of burglaries, 42 percent. The West reported twenty-three percent. The Midwest reported 21 percent. The Northeast faired best with 14 percent.

Sixty-five percent of all burglaries were by forcible entry. Twenty-eight percent were by unlawful entry, either through an open door or window where force was not needed or used.

Seven percent were reported as attempted forcible entries where an attempt was made but the burglar was frightened off.

If you arrive home and it appears that you may have been burglarized, do not go in! Go to neighbors or anywhere there is a phone and call the police. If you have a cell phone with you, still go to a neighbor's or somewhere safe to make your call. Your first concern is safety and that means to get out of the area. Your job isn't to catch anyone. It would be nice to see a face or to get some type of evidence but that's not the main issue...*your safety is. Go and get safe and call.*

Times of Vulnerability

Most burglaries occur during the day when most people are working, however, some happen in the afternoon and at night. Rapes and sexual assaults occur when the lady of the house is apt to be at home which is more likely in the evening or at night. These times of course vary with individuals' life and time schedules. Some women are home during the day, being stay at home moms, while some others may work non-traditional work hours such as shift work.

Keep Prying Eyes Away

The less information a burglar may have about your home the better. Close your blinds at night and consider closing them during the day. The less "he" can see from the outside the less control a predator has, and the more he now needs to be concerned with. Plus he can't window shop or be overly tempted by what you may have.

ALARM SYSTEMS

When most people think of home security they think of an alarm system or a dog. They are both good measures. An alarm system can be a fantastic security tool for your home and they have become increasingly popular. I wholeheartedly recommend them, one that is a good quality system and one that covers all the avenues of entry into your home.

One statistic I heard was that about *70% of unsuccessful burglaries were attributed to the alarm system scaring away the intruder.* Wow, that says a lot for all of us! When getting a system do not skimp on it because of cost if you do not absolutely have to. To alarm just one door and two windows as some people and companies tout just does not make much sense to me. Also, get the alarm system monitored by a central monitoring system that calls the police when the alarm is tripped. This is where alarm companies make their money. However, they offer a good service by monitoring your home. Just as importantly, I recommend that you also have an external siren attached to the outside of your home. Alarm systems usually come standard with an internal siren. This lets you and the intruder know that your alarm has been tripped but it does not let your neighbors know.

Alarms can be bypassed or compromised by some criminals. This compromising of your alarm can result in the signal not reaching the police. So to have an alarm that notifies *you and your neighbors* is a feature that I highly recommend. The louder and more annoying the siren is, the better. The idea is for your neighbors to hear the alarm and either come to your house to see what's up or to call the police. This is a time when a nosy neighbor is a good neighbor.

Technology is advancing daily and there may be new technological advances or features that your alarm representative can tell you about that fight against the average burglar from being able to defeat your alarm. One is a cellular backup for alarm systems that severely limit the average burglar from getting to you. This feature costs extra but it's truly a secure measure that severely limits the average burglar getting by your system.

You certainly want to get a reputable company to install your home alarm. I recommend a company that has a good track record and uses in-house company technicians, not outside contractors to do their work. Call your Better Business Bureau or ask your friends and associates if they could recommend a good alarm company. A call to your local police department may also be helpful in finding a reputable company.

CANINE PROTECTORS

Another important aspect that should be considered for home security is a dog. Some police officers feel that having a dog is a better security tool than an alarm system.

A burglary detective from a major metropolitan police department was quoted as saying "dogs are better to have than an alarm system for people who are concerned with home security." I do not necessarily agree with her statement but it has merit. This particular detective worked for a large urban department where the police response time was not the greatest. Factoring in the average time it takes for your alarm to reach the attention of a central alarm monitoring station and then having that station notify your local department can take five or six minutes or sometimes longer. Adding a slow local police response time, let's say of fifteen minutes or more, gives a ton of time for someone to burglarize your home or to do even worse.

A dog, on the other hand, is most always at your home watching and barking if someone comes near. Most predators will not want to chance dealing with a large or tenacious dog. The Los Angeles Police Department's Threat Management Unit says, "a dog is one of the least expensive but most effective alarm systems."

The big question that comes up is what kind of dog do you want. For the average person a dog is a companion, friend and family member. It is not a warrior dog ready to lay its life down for you. Most people do not want a killer type dog to guard them. However, well-bred and trained guard dogs do not have to be "monster" dogs. They can be friendly to family and friends and yet be a nightmare on four legs to the burglar or rapist breaking into a home.

There are many breeds that are well suited for home protection. To name some: Bull Terrier, Rottweiler, Akita, Boxer, Giant Schnauzer, Doberman Pinscher, German Shepherd and some different Mastiff breeds. The order they're listed has absolutely nothing to do with their merit as protectors.

Although, I must emphasize that these dogs must be bred well, they must come from the right stock, and they must be trained well. Then, of course certain mixed breed dogs can be well suited also.

The Rottweiler and Bull Terrier have had a great deal of bad press in recent years. If these dogs come from good stock and are trained well, they not only can be, but are excellent family pets and excellent protectors for you and your loved ones. Proper breeding and training are the keys for these breeds as really with all breeds.

The danger with improper breeding and training for a strong powerful breed of dog can be disastrous to you, your family and others. Of course, an improperly bred small Pomeranian could not cause anywhere near the same kind of damage to a person as an improperly bred or trained Rottwieler. Again, when choosing a dog, proper breeding and training is absolutely necessary.

The popular dog breeds such as the Labrador or Golden Retriever and some similar breeds may also be a good enough dog to keep burglars or predators away and possibly even physically protect you. I have seen first-hand a Labrador Retriever fearlessly protecting its master when a group of police officers entered a home trying to arrest its owner. The dog fearlessly held its ground until gunfire erupted.

Dogs not only can be used for protection but also as a warning system. Their hearing is great and in some cases downright phenomenal. They can let us know someone is nearby and we in turn can prepare ourselves or call the authorities. Small breed dogs and virtually all breeds of dogs can be used as a warning device for us. A warning device alone can make us feel more comfortable, not to mention more aware of what may be going around outside. A bad guy may not get nervous when he hears a small dog bark but he very well may back off fearing that the owners are aware, and possibly ready for him and in turn he may go elsewhere, somewhere *easier*.

A trip to the library or bookstore can give you more detailed information on the breeds that I mentioned along with some others that are preferred for actual physical home or personal protection. If you are considering a dog to help you in your home security needs, I highly recommend that you talk to a reputable animal trainer or at the bare minimum, do investigative reading on the right animal for you.

A concern with having certain breed dogs as pets is that some, if not all insurance companies, have restrictions or out and-out will not offer homeowners insurance to families with these dogs.

If you are presently insured and you purchase a dog such as a German Shepherd, which is a breed on certain lists as a restricted breed, and your homeowners contract does not specify that you have to notify them of any new dogs, you should be all right if you have to file a claim. By all right, I mean if for some reason the dog bites someone and you file an insurance claim, they would pay the claim.

If you're thinking of changing your homeowners insurance coverage to another company, it's most likely that the newer forms that you would need to fill out would specifically ask about what dogs you own. Owning certain breed dogs may stop the company from insuring you. An insurance expert tells me that insurance companies can also offer a "dog bite exclusion" clause in your contract, which means that they would insure you normally, but exclude any claim if your dog harmed someone. Another possibility is that if you have had a good record with a company, and the agent knows you as a responsible homeowner and your dog or dogs are "good" dogs, the company also may insure you.

I wholeheartedly recommend that you talk to an insurance expert or agent and ask about your specific situation. Rules, policies and procedures can change often and different cities, states or areas may do things differently, so ask about your personal circumstances.

Just as with alarm systems dogs can be defeated or circumvented. I worked on a burglary case, years ago where there was a thief who burglarized over 100 homes. At one home there was a large breed dog that the homeowner kept as a pet. During the day when most people are at work the burglar looked in the homes' windows and saw that the dog was confined to just a few rooms in the house. The burglar forcibly entered the home from another entrance and burglarized the rest of the home not accessible to the dog. This was a pretty gutsy move, huh? In another case a Doberman Pincher was shot by automatic gunfire as it came to defend the well-to-do homeowners during a daring nighttime home robbery. In the later example the alarm system the homeowner had was either not put on or was turned off from the inside by someone who had access to the home. The point here is that nothing is perfect or one hundred percent. What we can do is try to minimize our risks and yet live a comfortable enjoyable life.

Trimming Trees and Bushes and Lighting

Making the outside of your home safe is also an important aspect of a total home security plan or package. Trimming large bushes near windows and doors are paramount. These areas left unattended can give a prospective burglar or predator hiding places to break into windows or doors. They can take their good old time trying to get into your home. They don't have to worry as much about being seen by passersby or neighbors.

Having large bushes or untrimmed trees near your home can also give a prospective criminal a hiding place to wait for you when you come home. As you're walking into your home, someone hiding in that blocked or secluded area can jump out and get you. Some people plant prickly or thorny shrubbery near windows to discourage loitering or hiding. That's not a bad idea. So, it is important to keep the area near our homes neat and unobstructed.

Outdoor lights are also an important part of having a secure outer area. A well lit home makes it harder for the bad guy to hide in the darkness of your yard. It makes the area uninviting. You can also feel more secure when pulling into your driveway at night and being able to see your home and those possible hiding places where someone could be lurking. *Lights are your friends when it comes to safety and security.*

Having motion detector lights in your yard that go on automatically as your car pulls close to your home is an absolutely great security device. These motion detector lights are inexpensive and can be adjusted for their sensitivity. That is to say that by a simple turn of a dial or a knob you can adjust the distance for when you want the lights to go on. These lights will go on for a few minutes every time anyone or anything comes into the "distance" area that you have preset. This means if a person walks by the area, the light goes on. These lights make it so much easier for you to see your yard and home as you are pulling into your driveway or garage. They also make it uncomfortable for a bad guy to walk in your yard. Bad guys do not want to be seen and anything you can do to make them visible is outstanding. *Most intruders, some experts believe, will choose not to enter a home that is well lit.* Again, the trimmed bushes, which causes a lack of hiding places along with the well lit yard, all make it *less comfortable and just plain harder* for a predator to do his thing.

There are many different lighting schemes that can be used for the outside of your home. From the regular plain lights that are known to most people, to spotlights or to motion detector lights, all should be seriously considered for home security and at the bare minimum some should be utilized. They can be placed in a way that add beauty along with safety to your house.

Knowing Your Neighbors

Getting to know your neighbors is a great tool in your overall home security plan. When you get to know your neighbors they pretty much know when you come and go and what cars come and go in your yard.

One afternoon a man called the police and wanted to report a problem he was having with continuing harassing phone calls. It was a cloudy mid afternoon day as I was dispatched to the call. I pulled into his driveway, got out of my cruiser, walked up to the man's house and knocked on the front door. Shortly, an elderly man answered the door and greeted me. As he was introducing himself his phone started ringing, it was a neighbor across the street who saw my police car turn into his driveway. The neighbor was worried and wanted to make sure everything was all right with him. I'm sure that if I had been an unusual or suspicious car the neighbor would have called the police. What a great security measure this man had going for him…and it was free!

To get along with your neighbors to the point of them keeping an eye out for you is fantastic. Hopefully, you have neighbors that are "OKAY," and if so, get to know them and be a part of an unofficial "mini-neighborhood watch program."

In most cases you do not even have to ask a neighbor to watch out for you and your property. If you have a neighborly bond between each other they will tend to do it on their own.

Some good ways to get to know your neighbors are:

- Say "Hi".
- Take a walk and say a few words to them if they're out and about.
- Offer or ask for help.
- Share your garden bounty.
- Participate in neighborhood events.
- Welcome new neighbors with a greeting or an offer of a helping hand.
- Wave as you drive by.
- Be friendly; remember you have to live around them for a long time.

When going away on a trip and you have a trusting bond, you can:

- Ask neighbors to get your mail and newspapers.

- Give them a contact number for you.

- Give them names of friends or relatives and their phone numbers to contact in case of an emergency at your house while you're gone.

Or if you prefer, when going away, you can have your mail and newspaper held...but doing this broadcasts that you're leaving to a fair amount of strangers. It's better to have trusted neighbors or family taking care of these important issues.

Doors, Windows, and Other Points of Entry

The last thing I'm going to mention about home security is also the most obvious. Lock all your windows and doors. It sounds so simple but yet day in and day out I came into contact with people who did not lock their doors at night.

In today's age no matter where you live you should lock your doors. Any window that can be reached by someone also must be locked. Sliding glass doors should have a separate metal or wood pole that keeps the door from being opened relatively easily by a criminal. These poles usually lay in the inside track of where the door slides back and forth. A simple piece of wood cut in the right length does a good job. *This is an absolute must for security conscious people with sliding glass doors.*

There are also other security locking systems (other than just the basic doorlock) that are available for sliders. Sometimes these come installed with high quality slider-doors. There are also auxiliary locks that can be installed after the door is already in your home that will prevent the door from being opened or lifted out of its track, which is the big concern with sliders.

Good *deeply set dead bolt locks* should also be utilized. From sliders to doors to windows, anything that can give access to your "cave" should have a quality lock to keep you secure.

There are good locks for your windows that you can have installed other than the ones we all are familiar with. Window bars, the thick metal bars that definitely will keep the "bad guy" out are options and in the right circumstance or area may be the lock for you to buy. These are actually thick metal bars similar to the jail type ones that work great. The good ones can be opened from the inside with a key in case you need to get out quickly, like in case of a fire.

However, there are other visually pleasing quality windows and locks that can help you feel secure, and make you safer. A reputable locksmith or window manufacturer representative can help you with all your window lock concerns.

Locking Doors

I am amazed that people leave their doors unlocked. Open your eyes before it's too late. They are called locks, they were invented to lock things, and they are installed in homes to lock them, so lock up.

When I first became a policeman there was a rash of burglaries in a particular neighborhood. What the burglar would do at night was to walk through the area and just check to see if doors were unlocked. Any home that happened to be unlocked he would enter and burglarize, while the people were sleeping. He never burglarized a home where the doors were locked…never. This went on for quite some time and he was never caught. Thankfully, no one was ever hurt. Could you imagine if this individual's agenda was not burglary but something violent instead?

You may say yes, this was probably in a bad neighborhood. Not even close, this happened in a crime-free, safe area. Apparently, the people did not feel the need to lock up at night. *Do not make the same mistake.* We live in a mobile society where a relatively short drive can take people to good neighborhoods. So, if you live in a great neighborhood a bad guy might have to drive twenty or thirty minutes maybe to get from his "bad" neighborhood to you. However, don't be surprised that in your "good neighborhood" there are some predators trying to do their things. Needless to say, of course if you happen to live in a good neighborhood you can be assured some predators are pretty much going to think, hey, good neighborhoods have good stuff. They have good cars, good jewelry, etc. They are going to come and visit. I've seen it.

There was a brazen car thief who showed up once or twice a week in a great neighborhood and stole cars at night. The thief would enter unlocked garages and homes and find car keys that were usually easy to locate. He then stole cars, nice cars like BMWs, Cadillacs, Volvos and Jaguars. The cars were usually found the next day in a "bad neighborhood." This went on for a few months. Finally, the police caught the wily thief. He was a juvenile from that "bad neighborhood." He had a lengthy criminal record, and in this case, he just loved driving all those nice cars. He was kind of like taking test-drives, if you will.

Being a juvenile, they let him out while awaiting trial. Now do you know what he did while he was out? He went back to that same neighborhood and stole some more cars, and still, from unlocked homes. This was after tons of publicity in newspapers and television about the local thefts. People still did not lock up!

In another incident a woman was concerned that her neighbor who lived a few doors down from her, whom she described as "bizarre and frightening," might have stolen something from her house while she had stepped out. She told me that she had a young child and was concerned that this bizarre neighbor may do harm to her as well. While explaining her concerns she mentioned she felt he was bizarre for a long period of time before this incident occurred.

I asked her how this guy could have stolen the item that was missing; was there a broken window she noticed or a kicked-in door? She told me that he could have just walked in. "I don't lock my doors." Now wait a minute, she thought the guy was bizarre and had thought it for a long period of time before the apparent theft. Let's go on here...she is and has been frightened about him for a long time and she has a young child she's worried about. What am I missing? Lock your doors to start with!

If you leave your car in your driveway and you have an electronic garage door opener in the car, you may want to bring it into your house. It is relatively easy to break into your car and having your garage door opener gives the bad guy an edge in getting into your home. *About ten percent of illegal entries are gained through a garage door.*

Do You Know Where Your Keys Are?

Do not give keys to workmen or tradesman. They can easily make copies. If you're going to use a carwash and the attendants will have possession of your keys, remove your house key and *only give them the car key.* It's possible for them to easily make copies of your house keys and gain your home address from your license plate. Not only that, do not leave mail or other address information in your car like in the glove compartment, visor or laying on seats. Doing so, can make it easy for someone who may take a fancy to you to have easy access to where you live. This information holds true for when using a valet service also, leave only the car key and do not leave easy identifiers for anyone.

Keeping Safe and Secure When You Move

When you move into rental property or buy a new house *make sure one of the first things you do* is change the locks on all external doors. Anything less, to say the least, could be dangerous.

The Bedroom

We're all most vulnerable when we are sleeping and if you follow some of the sound security tips I've mentioned, you could rest your head with comfort knowing you've done some positives in you and your families security. However, there are certain materials you should also have with you in your nighttime haven, the bedroom.

• A cell phone in case you need to make a call and the phone line is out.

• A flashlight that can be used for illumination and also as an impact weapon if needed (we'll talk about weapons later.)

• A good deeply set dead bolt lock in the bedroom that you can lock in case you realize that someone is in your home. This room could be your "safe room" as well as your childrens if you happen to realize you have an intruder, from there you can call the police.

• Emergency telephone numbers.

• Pepper Spray, if you have made the decision to have this type of tool.

• Handgun, if you have decided to commit to its use as a tool for you.

Harassing Phone Calls

There is nothing much worse for women than getting a sexually harassing or threatening phone call late at night. When people make those harassing sexual calls they want shock/and or a reaction from you. You must not give it to them. Do not talk at all. Immediately hang up. If they call back, again do not talk or respond to anything they may say. *They want a response; do not give it to them.* Eventually, they will call someone else because they are not getting what they want from you.

Another type of call, such as someone threatening you and they seem to know private information about you or your family, should be referred to your local police department along with your local phone company. Don't get me wrong; you can still call the police on sexual or harassing calls, of course, but if they know personal things about you, call the police for sure.

Phone companies have a department called an Annoyance Bureau, or something similar, to deal with problem calls. The phone company can put a "trap" on your phone that shows them who the calls are coming from. When you go this route they will more than likely ask you to keep a log of every time the person calls you. *Keeping a specific log in any harassment situation is a positive, helpful thing to do.* It can provide crystallized information to authorities or investigators at a later date. A log simply means writing down the dates, times and specifics about your harassment or harassing calls, and then saving your written documentation of the events.

If you are having problems with annoying calls that continue, consider changing your phone number and getting an unlisted number.

Do not give personal information to anyone over the phone you don't know. *Never tell anyone that you live alone.*

Being Away From Home

When you are not at home you want to make your residence look as if someone was there. You want, in a way, to create the illusion of activity.

You can buy at least two plug in timers for lamps and set them to run at different times. These timers will turn lights on and off for the preset times you set them for. You can also get timers for televisions and audio systems that can be timed to make it seem as if the home is busy.

An answering or voice-mail machine can also be a good item to have. I knew of some burglars who would case a house and when they thought no one would be at home they would go near to the house, like across the street. Then they called the home and let the phone ring. If someone answered they would just hang-up and leave the area. If no one answered they would let it ring and ring and ring. Then they would walk up closer to the house and listen to hear the phone ring through the doors or windows. They would listen to their own call ringing at the house and assume that if no one answered, no one was home. They then would break in. An answering machine makes that technique pretty much un-usable to the burglar. He could never really know if the calls are being screened or if the residents are actually not home. If you live alone and don't want callers to hear a female's voice on your machine, buy one that has a prerecorded message or have a male friend or relative record your outgoing message.

If you go on vacation or plan on being gone for an extended period of time another option may be calling your local police department and asking if they keep a vacant house list or a vacation watch list. Some departments have these lists and will keep an eye on your home while you're gone. Also, as suggested earlier in the getting to know your neighbors section make sure you have a friend, relative or neighbor get your mail and newspapers while you're gone for longer periods.

Domestic Violence

Help and protection regarding domestic violence has come a long way. For generations and generations many women lived with it day in and day out, in silence. It was an accepted way of life. Many thought if you caused disfavor to your husband, you would get hit, get physically assaulted. It was accepted.

Slowly, things changed and that accepted way of life and behavior lost its extreme tight stranglehold. Yet the violence was still occurring way too often. Plus in many cases women unquestionably did not have the right degree of protection from it.

From Tragedy Comes Relief

After the domestic-related murder trial of the famous football player-turned-actor, O.J. Simpson, who was charged with killing his wife, domestic violence awareness took a giant step forward. Not only did positive awareness come about but also new stronger protective laws came into effect across the country.

These laws give household members so much more protection and added ways to stop abuse. We now enjoy a new national viewpoint that says that domestic violence is wrong and will not be tolerated. Many feel the Simpson case was a fiasco and justice was not served when he was found innocent of the murder of his ex-wife. The murder and case were, however, the cause of the largest leap forward for women's domestic violence protection I have ever seen.

The sad fact, though, is that domestic violence is still occurring every day in our nation's homes. Wives, girlfriends and in some cases men are being abused by their partners. Alcohol and drugs seem to be a factor in many, if not most, domestic violence situations. If I were to take an informal count on what percentage of domestic violence calls I had responded to where alcohol or drugs had been a contributing factor, I would say around 80% if not even higher. Inhibitions drop; common sense and self-control sometimes go out the door.

What are women to do when confronted by violence or the threat of violence by their partners? You start by not accepting one iota of it from anyone! Now read this closely:

There is nothing you can do or say that merits someone hitting or beating you up. ***Nothing!*** *They can divorce you, leave you, or call the police on you. They do not, however, have the right to strike you.* You are not a child who needs to be disciplined. You are an adult and no one has the right to physically harm you short of for self-defense reasons. That is the first thing to know, believe and remember. It is the truth.

If domestic violence occurs to you, call the police. Do not let it slide one time without doing something about it. Usually people who commit these acts continue to abuse. Without psychological help these people are apt to re-offend.

Twenty-Five Years of Abuse

I once went to a domestic dispute complaint where a wife called the police on her husband for hitting her. While talking to the woman, who appeared to be in her mid-fifties, I asked if this was the first time she had been struck by her husband. She told me no and that he had been hitting her on and off for a long time. When I pressed her for what a long time meant, she told me for about 25 years. She said the first time was when she was pregnant with their first child. He threw her down the stairs. The abuse went on for twenty-five years! She waited too long to call. Although, the good news for her was that she finally *did* call. You must call the police and stop it immediately.

A Yo-Yo Romance

In another incident, an attractive, well-educated and successful woman was almost killed by her longtime boyfriend. She lived in a condominium that was a freestanding building with about 8 separate units in it. She was getting beat up badly one night and her neighbors heard the commotion and called the police.

The police arrived and could hear the assault actually occurring. However, the problem was that the front door was metal and could not be broken down by the two responding officers, who were two big strong guys.

Well, the women feigned being knocked out while her live-in boyfriend was on top of her, hitting her in the head. Thinking she was dead or knocked out, he got off of her. When he did, she jumped up and bolted to the front door and let an officer in. The officer rushed in and at gunpoint arrested the man. He was booked, convicted and sentenced to jail. She was saved. A few days after the incident, the woman told me personally, that if the police had not arrived when they did she was convinced that she would have been killed. Her face looked as if though she had gone 12 rounds with the heavyweight champion of the world.

After the ex-boyfriend served his jail time, I'm not exactly sure when, she started dating him again. They dated for a few years until she started having problems with him. She would call the police fearing that he was either hiding in her house or possibly somewhere in her yard. Her fear was that because she broke up with him he would want to harm her or her daughter. They broke up and the calls to the police stopped. Later, she went back with him again and then broke up once more. The calls to the police started up every time they got back together. The last I knew, they were broken-up. I lost touch with her, and I'm not sure what ever happened to her. My sincerest hope is that she along with her daughter is doing well.

Following some of the principles, tips and the general mental attitude I'm trying to convey thus far, would you have continued to date this man? This is a test question…and the correct answer is…**NO!**

Help is Around the Corner

There are wonderful support groups that help women in times of domestic problems and abuse. They may be able to relate to your personal situation from experience. They may *really know* what you are going through and feeling, and they may be able to offer you advice and enlightenment that can give you *relief.* Never give up and think that it can't get better for you or that you do not deserve living well. **NEVER!** There are also safe-houses available to give you and your children shelter if you need it. Your phone book or your local police can help you contact these organizations, which are staffed with caring people, most of whom are volunteers who really care. They can make a difference in your life.

What Children Should Do When Home Alone

A complete home security plan would not be complete without talking about kids and how to keep them as safe as possible in their home. It is so important to keep children safe and also to give them a feeling of safety and empowerment in their homes, it can help in instilling within them a feeling of security throughout their lives. By getting them *involved in being a part of their home security* you are doing just that, empowering them.

There was a series of incidents I knew of where a man would knock on front doors where female teenagers were at home. When the girls answered the door he would ask for directions, then he would grope them. He then just simply ran off. This happened in several different communities and as far as I know this bizarre individual had not been caught. At the very least this case is weird, but true and definitely concerning. All across the country unusual or weird things *do occur* and importantly, there are some tips that children who are at home alone should heed:

- Do not open the door if the person is a stranger. Talk through the door if there is a need to find out what the person wants.

- If the person asks for help; tell him or her you will call the police, because an officer can provide assistance.

- If something happens, immediately call 9-1-1 so police can respond. If parents or relatives are called first, the suspect could be gone from the area by the time police arrive.

Children crave direction and are receptive when we tell them a true, positive, helpful course of action. Simple rules such as mentioned above can not only protect children, but can also give kids a feeling of being active in taking control of their lives, and starting them on the path of self reliance. Help them to have faith in you and ultimately themselves.

3

Being Safe While On the Go

It's a nice feeling to know that we have worked toward making some real meaningful steps in making our homes safe and secure. We come home and feel a sense of calm, knowing we've done some real positive steps for our families and ourselves.

Being away from home has its own challenges for women, challenges that can be met head on with knowledge and the commitment to be safe.

Being Safe While On the Road

Road Rage has been a hot topic for the last few years all across the country. Road Rage is when a driver of a vehicle basically "flips out" due to being jammed up in traffic, being given the finger or cut off by another driver. When I say flip out I mean individuals ram other cars with their own, beat people up, shoot at other drivers and sometimes even kill them. This is such a problem throughout the country that some police agencies actually have had special units that look for enraged drivers. They target vehicles that are tailgating, cutting off other cars, and other actions that can be behaviors of someone in the stages of road rage.

In Akron, Ohio a taxi driver shot and killed another driver, who was angry that the taxi driver committed a traffic violation that inconvenienced, or bothered him. Words were exchanged and the other car's driver walked up to the taxi and punched the driver's side window, shattering the window onto the taxi driver. The taxi driver said that he thought his window had been shot out by the enraged driver. At this point, he pulled his handgun out that he said he carried for self-protection and shot the other man, killing him.

This all happened over some traffic problems that had escalated. The taxi driver was carrying a handgun illegally and was convicted for that in court. However, he was found criminally not guilty for the killing of the man. The jury accepted his self-defense explanation.

The reality is that many people carry firearms illegally and will use them. So when driving, keep in mind that you do not know whom the person is that you may be in the midst of having a problem with. You have no idea, and that safe comfort feeling that a car can give you can be shattered quickly. Do not get involved in the Road Rage game. If someone cuts you off or does something similar that really bothers you, try to just get away from the situation. Let it go and be on your way. Stay away from the finger pointing and hollering that can start up. Let it go; you will be better off.

To make matters even worse, some men feel a sense of power over women. In a road rage situation they sometimes will go at it with an extra vigor, by tailgating and similar behavior, because they feel a sense of advantage over women. They feel less physically threatened so some take advantage and go all-out in their abuse and road rage actions against women…more so than they would a man driver. Simply put, *do not get involved.*

Don't Get Carjacked

A car jacking occurs when someone approaches you while you are either getting into your car or while you are driving. They may approach your car at a red light, stop sign or a parking lot. They usually threaten you with a gun or a knife and either hop in your car, sit next to you or, tell you to get out of the car. Then they hijack, or in this case, car-jack your vehicle.

If they want you to get out of the car, that is preferable than hopping in next to you. If they hop in next to you, you could lose a lot more than just your car.

• Again, be aware of your surroundings.

• Be aware of not getting boxed in. Some robbers have been known to box people in on roadways, more or less locking cars in place, making it difficult in escaping their criminal intent. They work as a team where one car works to get in front of you and the other car behind you. When they have you "boxed in" where they feel you can't pull out and away from them, someone gets out and tries to get into your car. It's best to try to give yourself some "wiggle room," so you can pull forward or backwards when stopped, if need be. You do this by attempting to always see the *rear tires* of the car in front of you and by being aware. Be aware of any attempts to box you in, if you see one; pull away to the front or back, whatever works.

• If approached by a man wielding a gun demanding you let him in, don't do it, pull away as fast as you can while keeping your head down. It's unlikely that he really wants to shoot you or for that matter can actually hit you if he did shoot. I will talk more in depth about this in the section on getting in attacker's cars in Chapter 6.

- If you do get carjacked make sure you have your seat belts on, most likely the carjacker won't. Slam your brakes on, hard and at a fairly high rate of speed, where he'll get thrown into the windshield whereas you won't. Then, in the confusion, get out of the car and run.

- If by chance you get carjacked and are put in the trunk, look around for a pull down lever, that some cars have that open the trunk from the inside. If you find such a lever or cable, wait until the car comes to a stop and open the trunk and run. If there isn't a latch, search the entire trunk for wires and rip them out, *all of them.* You may engage the power trunk release; disengage the fuel-pump or possibly disengage some of the running lights that may bring the car to the attention of a policeman.

Be aware of the type of neighborhood you're driving in to set your level of awareness. As safely as possible, run a stop sign or a red light if you are being approached in a suspicious manner. Keep valuables out of sight, and by all means **always** have your car doors locked while driving. When a woman gets in a car, the first thing she should do is lock her doors. *Get into the habit of doing it every time, just like putting on a seat belt.*

Some people may have a concern about locking car doors, then fearing the possibility of getting into an accident, becoming unconscious or incapaci-tated…their concern being that it might be difficult to extricate one from a car. It's relatively easy to break a car window and some policemen actually carry an item called a "window punch" for just such occasions. They hold it up next to a window and press a lever and presto the window shatters. Although, even the average passerby should be able to break your window if the need arises, so *lock your doors.*

One afternoon there was a terrible accident in front of my house where a young driver was trapped in an overturned car. Passersby, one of which was a construction worker at my house, kicked a window out and helped the man out of the car.

Do not pick up hitchhikers, and if someone looks like he needs help with his car, do not pick him up. Get help by making a call for him or by notifying the police. Similarly to what I mention later on in the book about the subject, if you want to be a Good Samaritan, be one, but be one by being smart. *The few minutes that it may take you to make a call or summon help will most likely not cause harm to that stranded motorist.*

Once while patrolling, I stopped to help a man who was fixing a flat tire on a roadway one night. He ended up having warrants for his arrest out of Colorado for Kidnapping Using Violence, along with some additional assault warrants. When I first started talking to him he sounded like the nicest guy around. Something about him seemed fishy to me and I had a thorough computer record check done on him while on the roadway. Lo and behold, serious warrants popped up. I arrested him, and a few days later Colorado authorities flew to Ohio and took him away. Help, but help by not getting too close where you can possibly be "caught."

If someone pulls alongside of you pointing at your car as if something is wrong with it, do not pull over with him. Go to a safe area. *There's nothing likely that is going to happen to your car that can't wait.* Women have fallen for this ruse and have been assaulted. Take your time and calmly evaluate.

The Safety in a Telephone

Cell phones are great things for women to have and are great gifts for teenage girls to receive if not for any other reason but for security. It's also a great idea to have a cell phone with you while driving. It can definitely come in handy to summon help if you should need it. *Cell phones are a must for women's security.*

Everyone knows about dialing 911. With a cell phone you can dial 911 just as with traditional landline telephones. Although, there is no guarantee that the police will be able to find you if you do, at least not quickly, but they *will find you.* When you dial 911 from your home telephone, which uses regular phone lines, most likely an Enhanced 911 system, will take your call. Most emergency call centers use an Enhanced 911 system that shows the location of where the call is coming from. Not so with a cell phone. Only about 40% of emergency agencies are able to locate wireless calls. Mathematical formulas or global satellite positioning are needed to locate wireless transmission locations. It can be done, you can be located, but the idea of 911 for you, is the quickest knowledge of your location so you can get immediate help.

What is helpful when using 911 with your cell is to know where you are, if not exactly, generally. You will need to tell the operator at minimum where you general location is.

I realize that while driving, particularly long distances, it is difficult to keep track of where you are. Keep it in the back of your mind, that when you travel and might have to rely on your cell phone dialing 911, you have to have an awareness of your location. Here we are again, awareness. Not hyper aware, *just aware.*

Flat Tires Do Not Have To Be THAT Scary

If you get a flat tire in a bad area, don't have a cell phone and you feel uncomfortable getting out of the car to fix the tire, then ride the flat tire. Drive the car on the flattened tire, and if need be on the rim until you can get to an area where you feel safe to get some help. Any damage to the rim is only money.

I once saw an intoxicated man who drove on two flat tires for so long that he was driving totally on metal rims kicking up tons of sparks as he drove. Another policeman and I happened to notice him late one night and after taking a double take, stopped him. The man was in his early sixties and was a friendly sort of guy who didn't think he was doing anything unusual. He told us that he only had about twenty more miles to drive to get home. Now, I don't mean to sound insensitive to the problem of drunk driving (I have received several awards for D.U.I. enforcement) when I tell you that I was laughing so uncontrollably about what he had done and how normal he thought it was, but I just couldn't stop from laughing, laughing and then laughing some more. I'm lucky he was a nice guy and didn't try to get the drop on me, he probably could have. However, he was a nice guy and I learned something that night…that a car can be driven without tires for a long, long time.

Again, it's only money if you need to drive on a flat and damage is the cause. *You should also carry a Fix-A-Flat type can in your vehicle.* It may keep you safe and healthy and of course that's way more important. These cans hook up to a flat-tire stem and when you push the aerosol can button it re-inflates the tire and seals the puncture for a good period of time. This is an excellent, helpful item to keep with you. They are easy to use and *you shouldn't pull out of your driveway without it.* You can buy these cans just about anywhere and they work. I know; I've used them.

With new technological advances there are new advances in all kinds of areas. There are even new tires that have been developed that can experience a large puncture and still be driven for miles and miles. Also, a new gel has been developed that is inserted into a tire and it stops a tire from deflating when punctured. These are great new advances that are available and can be utilized by not only women, but by everyone. These are new and possibly not quite ready for major distribution but the next time you're in the market for tires ask your sales representative.

Accidents

If you get into an accident and feel concerned that you're at physical risk, drive to a safe area and call the police. Criminals have been known to cause an accident just to have the other driver get out so they can rob or assault them. *If in doubt, go to a safe area.*

When Getting Cash

Our security at ATMs is a concern for many of us, and rightly so. I'm 6 foot 1 and hover around two-hundred and fifteen pounds and when I walk up to an ATM I still wonder if there is someone waiting to help himself to my cash. If someone really needs money, the enviable green stuff, where can they get it? An ATM spits money out; the stuff some predators desperately want to get their hands on. It's actually a money machine for God's sake and a heck of a temptation to some.

Think about it, what better way is there for a criminal who is so inclined, to get some free cash other than this scenario. He watches a person walk up to a relatively secluded machine, knowing almost positively that they will be taking out untraceable cash and putting it in their purse or wallet. All this bad guy has to do is watch for the *right person* to walk or drive up to an ATM. Then they make their move at the right time, and boom, they have your money. The problem is that sometimes they not only take your money but sometimes also your car and your life.

So what do we do? Again, we should keep in mind that the bad guy is most likely looking for the easiest target. I recommend using a drive-up ATM if at all possible but if that's not feasible, use the strategies we discussed earlier about how to present and carry yourself. ATMs in crowded areas are great to use. With more secluded ones, before you walk up, look around for dark or sheltered areas where someone could be hiding. Approach the ATM when there are people around if possible. If something or somebody looks strange to you, do not approach. Go elsewhere.

I listened to an interview of a young man who was convicted of an ATM robbery of a woman who was also abducted and killed. The robber/killer who was one of three who were convicted of the crime was remorseful after his conviction. He said that he felt terrible about what he was involved in. He talked about what he would recommend for men and women using ATMs. He said people should be aware of their surroundings, to look for anything unusual or suspicious. He went on to say that people have to keep a lookout...that they have to be aware of what may be out there. He said about his victim, *"that if the woman would have been more aware and concerned about her surroundings, she might be alive today."*

This is one of the most important things you'll read in this book. People who are concerned with their safety around ATMs and everywhere should take his comment as gospel. This information came from the horse's mouth. *Be concerned and aware of your surroundings.*

There are tons of ATMs; they have sprouted up like weeds. If you're approached at one in a robbery attempt and someone demands your money, drop the money and get out of there at the same time. Drop or throw the money and take off. His main priority will be the cash and if you leave it there for him and run away this could be your best bet. Cash, of course, is replaceable, you're not.

Do not conduct any banking transaction other than what is really necessary, in this case, getting the cash you need. Do not pay bills or look up balance information or any other transaction at an ATM that is even semi-secluded or at night. If there are people around and the atmosphere is one of safety and security, by all means, go ahead, but anything short of a safe atmosphere, don't do anything that isn't essential, and then do that quickly.

If you're in a car pulling up to an ATM, be aware of your surroundings and again if something looks strange, go elsewhere. Also be aware of being boxed in. This means that you pull up behind a car that you believe is doing a transaction when another car pulls up behind you. They are working together and box your car in. You are "locked in" backwards and forward. To minimize this, as discussed in the earlier car jacking section leave yourself some wiggle room. Leave a space between the cars that you pull behind if possible, enough of a space to get out fast if needed. If you do get boxed in and feel you have the ability to ram your way out, ram out in reverse not forward. The odds are that you have air bags in your car and if you collide with someone from the front, the bags will engage and at the minimum, cause obscured vision and possibly throw you out of a confident mindset.

Being boxed in is probably a rare occurrence at ATMs but it is something to keep in the back of your mind. I generally do not recommend the ram solution; however, if you feel that you have the space between vehicles to get enough torque and you have the sense or intuition that you can make it work, go for it, and ram your car out fast and hard. You can, of course, use the ramming move anywhere you may be boxed in by vehicles.

I wholeheartedly recommend keeping your car in gear with your foot on the brake while doing your transactions at all drive up ATMs. Keep aware and if someone approaches your car, simply take your foot off the brake, give the car some gas and pull away.

When Shopping

Shopping's usually an exiting and fun time for most women. They anticipate walking into the local mall or shopping center thinking about what great buys they may find.

In the last few years shopping malls have concentrated greatly on beefing up their indoor, and more importantly, their outdoor parking lot security. One reason this was done was because of lawsuits filed by crime victims who had been assaulted, raped and robbed while in the area of malls. Malls across the country were being held responsible for the safety of their shoppers.

In many malls or shopping centers you'll see roving security patrol cars with their overhead police type lights on, patrolling the parking lots. There are numerous other security measures malls across the nation are using. This is only good news for all of us shoppers. However, this does not mean that shopping at malls or shopping centers is risk free. Nothing could be further from the truth. Nevertheless, of course the better security they have, the better your chances of going home safe and sound.

Areas where people shop also draw criminals that want to prey. Crime is an easier way to make a living for some predators.

To many of us, this way to make a living may seem a hard way to go. Not so, really. One of the "toughest" criminals I knew told me that criminals are not the real tough or hard guys. He said that it was easy to rob a woman or to prey on the weak. He went on to further say that it was tough to get up every morning and punch a clock or work 8-to-5 everyday. He told me that those people were the real tough guys. Similarly, for those of us who have gotten up day-in and day-out and worked steady for years or have worked long hours, we know that it *is* tough. It is a testament to our strength as responsible people.

A Real Eye Opener

Fairly recently, an Ohio fireman was convicted of rape and other charges and was sentenced to prison for probably the rest of his life. This in itself is not shocking news but what is shocking is what this man did in his quest to ravage women. After he was arrested, the police found literally thousands of names of women, whom he had literally catalogued, that he was looking into abusing.

He admitted to authorities that he would stand behind women who caught his fancy in checkout lanes and looked at either driver's licenses or checks that they were writing. He would also write down license plates of cars and get information on their owners. Or he would follow some of these women from the mall or grocery store to see where they lived. Once he found out where they lived, he would watch the home, sometimes for months. He would see if they lived alone and *if they had a dog*. It appears that this case was the biggest (by sheer volume of females involved) stalking case in our country's history. He not only stalked them, he sexually assaulted many of them.

He was finally caught because a woman whom he had been spying on for a long time, who lived alone, happened to have her big strong brother spending the night at her home one night. This predator broke into the home and was ready to do his thing. No alarm system, no dog, but OOPS, big brother happened to be sleeping on the couch that night. A fight ensued and the brother came out on top and held the man down until the police arrived.

Be cautious with your personal information; tell no stranger you live alone. You can glance in your rear view mirror at times to make sure that no one is following you. Women have special issues to deal with when it comes to survival. It's a shame, but its reality. That's all right, though. By following some of the guidelines talked about in this book *you can manage the unique challenges*.

A good way to keep personal information out of spying eyes is to not let people invade your space in stores or at a checkout lane. If someone is uncomfortably looking over your shoulder or is too close to you, *out and out stop it. Take no garbage, and speak up.* Stay aware of keeping personal information material away from prying eyes. Now, there's that word again, AWARE. A strong, unhappy look to someone invading your space may be enough to stop the activity, but saying something loud where others hear it may also be the correct course of action for you. It's not the time to be shy. Take no possible abuse or violation. You are not a victim and you will not be a victim. Do whatever you need to do to not be abused, hurt or taken advantage of, *period!* Trust yourself to do and say what is needed.

When someone appears to be invading your space, or who may be sizing you up, use the words "Back off". This is the preferred term to use which may result in your not becoming a potential victim. It's not confrontational yet it is assertive and shows that you are focused in strength if need be. It's an excellent term to use; keep it in mind.

A Good Neighborhood Offers Good Security

One of the first things you may want to consider is to look for the mall or shopping area that has a high presence of security officers/and or obvious security measures. Find one that is in an area known to be in a "good neighborhood," even if this means driving an extra half-hour or so. This sounds simple or may sound like an inconvenience to you but to search out the good area with good security can save a world of heartache for you and your loved ones.

Some may ask what I mean by a good neighborhood? Shouldn't we really not label areas as bad and give challenged areas a chance to flourish, and by labeling certain areas as "bad" aren't we causing a problem or disservice? Nonsense.

There are bad areas and dangerous areas. Stay away from them and you will be better off. This particular book is not about saving communities or attempting to be politically correct. That's for another book by another author. Of course I want every neighborhood to flourish and succeed in my country. There are workers, activists and professionals who are working on those issues every day throughout the country. This book's about another issue. Until some areas turn around and get safe, prudent people are not going to frequent them and *they should not. Avoidance of bad areas is a major key for the security conscious person.*

Stay Informed

Fairly close to where I live there is a large mall that was popular. At one time the mall was one of the largest in the country. As time went by there was a huge amount of crime being committed there and it got to be known to many as being a dangerous place to shop. Many police officers I knew told me that when they did shop there, they definitely took their off-duty handguns.

What struck me was that so many people still shopped at the mall, including tons of women, alone. Armed off-duty police officers did not really want to shop there and yet many women would go there alone. I think the average citizen or shopper did not know how bad the area was. If they had, I believe they would have gone elsewhere, which in my opinion would have been the prudent thing to do.

It is very important to know where you are shopping. Are there gangs or groups of youths hanging around without security nearby? *Read your local newspaper to keep up on your environment so you know what's going on around you. Be an informed woman.* If you still want or must go to a bad area, go early. *Bad guys generally stay up late and sleep in late. They generally like to do their thing later.*

PARK NEAR AND BE AWARE

Park as close to the entrance of a building as possible and walk inside with a group of people instead of alone. Simple but yet sound advice. The next time you are about to get out of your car in a mall parking lot, *slow down a little and ask yourself, should I look around a little? Should I wait a second and walk with others instead of just bolting out?* Or vice-versa when you're leaving the mall to go to your car, ask yourself, *Should I wait a second or two and walk with others?* Take the time to look for others who are walking into the mall and join in with the crowd or group. Remember the old cliché that there is safety in numbers; it is true.

At night, take the extra time to attempt to park in a well-lit area. Sure, it can be an inconvenience, but it's all a part of being aware of your surroundings. Let me say it yet in another way, being aware of *your particular surroundings* is one of the most important things you can do for yourself when it comes to your personal security.

How do you become aware of your surroundings? Simply open your eyes and *have the desire* to see what is going on around you. Are there people who look "funny" watching you? I use the term "funny" often in this book and by it, I mean concerning or different in an unusual or unhealthy way, that type of thing. Realize the consequences of not knowing your surroundings; these consequences can be devastating. Does something look out of the ordinary to you? Trust your instincts. Instincts are real; we all have them and in their most basic and natural sense they can be very helpful. Nature has endowed each of us with basic instincts. Then, of course the more we read, learn and experience, the more they become finely honed. I really mean trust yourself and your natural instincts. In most cases they will not let you down.

It is better to be safe than sorry. *If you think something looks strange or unsafe, go around it or go away from it.* A little inconvenience is all that it is, an inconvenience, a little time wasted. It is better than what can happen if we act foolhardily.

Exercise Reasonable Caution

When inside a shopping area, use reasonable caution.

- Keep your purse close to you and closed up.
- Do not show large sums of money when paying for items.
- Don't wear all of your expensive jewelry that someone may spot and mark you for his potential victim or meal ticket.
- Be careful with whom you strike up conversations. Good con men or thieves can be smooth and good at what they do.

When I was a Loss Prevention Manager for a national retailer there was a man who walked up to me while I was talking to some employees near a refund desk. I had a sport-coat and tie on and the man obviously figured me as some kind of manager. He may have actually known I was the Loss Prevention Manger. He asked if we could give him change for a one hundred dollar bill. He looked like the typical middle-aged, male shopper, overweight with a paunch, balding, dressed with clothes that came right out of suburban family-man's quarterly. However, it struck me as funny he would come up to me, not the obvious employee working the desk and flash a 100-dollar bill. I figured him to be a thief trying to show me that he was a man who did not have to steal. Well, it turned out the man was a professional thief and was attempting to steal hundreds of dollars worth of merchandise. He was a con, smooth, but this time just a little too much so.

So, be cautiously aware of who you are dealing with or with whom you strike up conversations, because sometimes people are not who they appear to be. Be your cautious, observing self and you will be able to discern.

Should You Help Others?

The man who the term "serial killer" was first used on was Ted Bundy. He often used false pretenses to get women to help or come with him. From using a fake arm cast preying on women's sympathy to lying about some tragedy that happened to a family member, he tried many things to trap women into his control. Then he devastated, raped and killed them. Be cautious helping anyone where you put yourself in possible danger. That's why God created cell phones. Make a call to help someone if there's any possibility of you getting into harm's way, instead of trying to help them yourself. It may take longer for the help to get to the man in need, but that's just the way it goes sometimes in the name of safety.

Better to be a Live-Helper Than A Dead-Hero

As an example, throughout my years in policing I've been at numerous fire calls, whether they were cars or trucks engulfed or houses or apartments ablaze. Quite often police arrive at the scene of fires way before the fire department does which was often the case for me; I seemed to arrive way before the professionals from the fire department did.

Most of the time I'd have fire extinguishers in the trunk of my police cars and quite often I'd rush up to the car, truck or house and try to put the fire out. Sometimes I actually put smaller fires out but one day a former firefighter turned police officer told me that I was acting foolishly by rushing in without oxygen or worse yet, walking into homes that were ready to explode, unbeknownst to me.

It might have been "brave" of me to go into these places but I wasn't properly equipped or trained for many of the areas I was going into or trying to get into. If I would have walked up to the wrong house that might have been on the verge of exploding as burning houses can do, to help someone and ended up killing myself, whom would I have helped? No one. Not only that, I wouldn't have been around to help the next person the next day with some other problem. I wouldn't have been around to help my family or experience my life any longer. So for you, if there's the possibility that you may get hurt in helping someone, *pause, think and call for help if you have doubt.* Don't try to be a hero, *be smart and still help.*

DO NOT WALK ALONE

I cannot emphasize how important it is to walk with others when walking to or from your car. As I said earlier there is safety in numbers and of course this means going to and from.

Several years ago there was an incident in the greater Cleveland area where a mother was shopping at a mall. The mall was considered safe, in a good area. The mother was with her two children and as they were leaving, she told her kids to wait in the mall near the exit while she went to get their van. It was a cold snowy day and she probably didn't want her children to have to walk to the car in the frigid Cleveland weather.

She never came back to pick her children up. The case was puzzling and was not solved for a long time. As time went by the police arrested two people for the kidnapping, rape and murder of the young mother. She was carjacked in the lot while she was getting her car to pick her kids up. She was also tortured and raped. She then was killed. Two young men were convicted and sentenced in the crime.

I don't know how she may have walked to her car that day and I will not second-guess her. However, at the bare minimum there is safety in numbers and you can utilize this sound security practice.

A horrible kidnapping incident that occurred in January of 2005 at a Texas Wal-Mart shocked the nation because it was caught on tape from an outside security camera. A female employee was leaving work in the evening and was going towards her truck in the parking lot. As the 19 year old neared her vehicle a man ran up behind her and shoved her into her truck and drove off.

Two days later, her body was found about 400 miles away. The apparent abductor, a man in a long, dark coat, was seen loitering around the front entrance of the Wal-Mart and was also seen on surveillance tape walking around inside of the store prior to the abduction.

The woman had been shot, most likely near where her body was found. The suspect later identified as a Johnny Lee Williams continued driving the girl's truck and attempted a robbery at an Arizona RV park. At the park, an employee carrying a handgun legally, foiled the robbery by pulling his gun as Williams said, "this is a robbery; I want all the money in the cash register" and pulled a weapon from underneath his shirt. When he pulled his weapon and said those words the employee drew his own gun and fired. Williams was taken into custody and treated for his gunshot wound. The employee was not charged in the shooting.

Hindsight is 20-20 and it's easy to pick apart mistakes looking back at a leisurely pace in a "perfect world." I do not want to do that in regards to this case either, but it can be useful to mention certain areas that may help someone else in a similar circumstance later.

- Employees or customers should speak up if they notice someone that looks suspicious or is "hanging around."

- Employees should seriously consider never going into a dark parking lot alone; store policy could state that a male employee will walk with every female upon evening departures (or a similar procedure).

- When leaving any area at night and you're alone, wait until some others are walking out and mix in with them. Remember clichés are clichés because they are true; and the cliché that says *there is safety in numbers*, is definitely true and extremely *important!*

- When walking, be aware as much as possible for people nearby or possibly behind you.

- When walking home as an example, walk facing traffic so a car cannot pull up behind you unnoticed.

- Consider carrying pepper-spray, ready at hand and ready for immediate use.

- Have your keys ready at hand to use as a sharp defensive weapon.

Remember to notify someone if you see something, or someone that seems concerning to you. In today's day and age sometimes we are afraid that we may seem too nosy or we may not be politically correct. Make it your business to get involved. *By speaking up you may save someone's life.*

Travel Safely

Staying at hotels can be a pleasant experience for some people and for others it can be an uncomfortable time. Sleeping in a strange bed as opposed to our familiar beds causes some of us discomfort. Personally, I'm a big baby and I like my own bed…but travel for many is a must. It's estimated that women traveling for business is around 25% of all business travelers. Hotel and motel stays cannot only be an uncomfortable experience, it can be a downright dangerous and in some cases, a tragic one.

NBC television's *Dateline* did an undercover investigation on hotels and motels. The crux of the investigation centered on what kind of job they were doing recovering keys from previous guests who did not return them upon checking out. In the event where keys are not returned, the lock for those particular rooms should be changed before the room is rented out to someone else. The investigation showed that in most cases the locks were not changed. This means the new renter was not the only one with a key for their little home away from home. A stranger also had a key. Knowing this sure would make it hard to get cozy and comfortable in your room wouldn't it?

Dateline reported that Mary Connelly and her son had checked into a motel in North Carolina and didn't realize that others, besides the desk clerk, might have had a key to their room. At least they didn't until they heard someone unlock their room door. "I hear someone turning the doorknob back and forth," says Mary, "so I picked my head up off the pillow, and with that the door opened up and this man came in. I said, "What do you want?" Then he says, "*Wake up call, wake up call, we're here to rob you.*" Now that's pretty funny, huh. No, it's pretty frightening! The police figured that the two men who robbed them that night had a key to their room.

Many hotels now use a card system instead of a key. You are given a card similar to that of a credit card and it's coded for your particular room. You simply swipe the card in the appropriate area on the door and the door unlocks. This is better than the standard key system. The code is changed or reprogrammed whenever a new renter is given a room. The truth of the matter is that any security system can break down, either by being defeated by criminals or just by simple human error. New technologies such as electronic keys or cards will probably lead to even more advanced technological breakthroughs. High-tech devices, however, are only as effective as the people who manage them.

The cornerstone to room safety is to always use the internal door locks that almost all hotels offer. A good inside dead-bolt lock along with a flip lock that many hotels have should *always* be utilized. These cannot be unlocked by anyone other than the person inside of the room. If it's a quality inside lock mechanism, it's a good security measure for you. If it is a cheap or flimsy one, demand another room with a strong secure lock. If the hotel only has cheap locks, get out and find another hotel, even if it means driving more to your seminar, relative's house or business meeting. Without having that good internal lock, do not tuck yourself in with a false sense of security.

Key locks, card locks and the like can all be compromised. Even the internal locks can be forced open by brute force. Although, if they are a strong, sturdy mechanism they are not an easy task to break down and importantly it would cause a lot of noise. This is something the bad guy does not want. Noise is not their friend.

Also importantly, use the peephole in the door that the hotel hopefully has. Some hotels do not have them, which may be a reason you should choose another one.

Of course they are there for you to see who is at your door, so don't forget to use it. If you have any doubts that the person behind the door is not whom you *know* them to be, call the front desk. Sometimes bad guys will knock on your door and say they are maintenance or some other hotel employee. *Do not believe them without calling the front desk and making sure that they have sent someone to your room.* Again, remember to use every internal lock the room has to offer, this includes any extra lock a sliding glass door may have.

Asking about the safety record of the hotel from friends, relatives or co-workers is always a good idea. They very well may have heard about incidents at the hotel that could be helpful to you. If you have concerns, call the local police department and ask them about the facility that you are thinking about using.

I recommend that you stay away from first floor rooms and rooms that are not an inside entry room. By inside entry I mean rooms that you have to walk into the hotel first, and from there, onto your room.

- Being on the first level, you may be too close to the possible pervert or thief who may be coming and going near entrances and exits in an unrestricted way. Also, your window is at or near ground level, making it easy to get into.

- Similarly, having an outside entry to your room makes it so much easier for the bad guys to give you trouble. You may want to ask for a room near the lobby or an elevator. Some people feel more comfortable being in eye-view of the lobby.

- A smaller hotel is better. A smaller lobby makes loiterers easier to notice for management. In a smaller hotel it's also easier for the staff to be familiar with you and legitimate guests.

Other things worth considering are listed below and in most cases can be asked in advance:

- Finding out if the hotel has twenty-four hour manned security or at least manned nighttime security.

- Do the doors that come from parking lots or areas where people off the street can get into the hotel other than by walking by the main desk, lock automatically after a certain hour?

- Ask hotel employees what security measures they have.

- Ask what kind of neighborhood it is. This can make you more aware of your particular surroundings. Hotels, similar to shopping areas, are finding they need to keep their customers safe.

That same *Dateline* show found a nighttime security officer sleeping in his car in the parking lot while he was supposed to be patrolling at a hotel. I bet he no longer works for the hotel and I bet the hotel now, is sensitive to having quality, accountable security. Hotels and motels are stepping up to the plate.

In hotels, it almost always seems that we are the only ones walking down hallways. Even if the hotel is filled to the brim, it quite often seems that when we walk to and from our rooms there is no one else around. This can and is an uncomfortable time for many people. Walk with confidence and above all be aware of your surroundings. Have your key in your hand as you're going toward your room; be conscious of where the exits are. *BE aware, there's no need to fumble at the door trying to find your key.*

There are two basic reactions to a threat, to run or to fight. Many species have survived for thousands of years because they have learned to run like the wind. Do not underestimate your running ability. To run to an exit and down a stairway toward the front desk, can be accomplished with the speed and agility of an Olympic runner, if you are in relative good health and are motivated. Plus, there is no better motivation than possible annihilation.

High heeled or cumbersome shoes can severely put a dent in your running ability. Either consider not wearing them at certain times or get ones that can be slipped out of in a snap. Do not sell yourself short on your ability to run down a flight of stairs as an example, by just about throwing yourself down the stairs in an almost controlled free fall type run. Yes, you may cut, bruise and even break something like a toe or finger, but you *can* make it and run to safety. Again, do not sell yourself short to be able to get yourself out of dangerous situations.

You must not freeze or hesitate. Go for it. If you have to run, run and scream. Make others aware that you need help. A bad-guy does not want to chase you down a lobby while you're running and screaming louder than a crazed fan at a football game. You can and will survive. People do it every day *and you're no different.*

When I was about twelve years old I was out with my friends on Halloween night, trick or treating. We had been out for a few hours and happened to go to a friend's house. My friend went into the house while I stayed alone on his front porch.

All of a sudden someone came up to me and put a gun to my head. He was at ground level while I was on the porch that had a solid stone railing about three feet high. He said something to the effect of give me all your candy or he would kill me. Yes, you read right, all your CANDY or he would kill me. I don't remember his face at all. I remember the gun vividly to this day. The moment he told me what he wanted, and what he would do to me, I immediately ducked down below the solid stone porch rail and almost simultaneously opened the front screen door and dove into the house, knowing there were adults inside.

I got away without being harmed. At that young age I felt that I could get away from the situation, I went for it, and it worked. A few minutes later another of my friends, Jerome, who happened to be down the street, was robbed, I'm sure by the same guy. Thankfully he only lost his candy. The area that I grew up in was in a transition period at that time and eventually turned into the highest crime area in the state of Ohio. This was over candy, not cash, gold or silver…unbelievable.

I was nothing really special, sure I had some martial art training under my belt by that time, and I had also been a crime victim years earlier. That very well may have unconsciously turned my survival juices up a notch or two and my general upbringing may have been positive in the area of surviving. However, you are not less than I am. You may not have had the same training, background or experiences that I had, but by reading this book and believing in the fundamentals I'm showing you, you've just gained much of what I had at that time and so much more because of the experiences and training I've garnered since then.

I'm no better than you are. You too can make it. You and I have a lot of unique abilities and strategies that we can use and use successfully. Have faith in your awareness and ability.

TRAINS, SUBWAYS AND SHIPS

Cruise ships have become extremely popular and train travel has seen periods of popularity. Doors should be locked immediately when you get into your room or cabin. Stay aware of your surroundings and use the people skills discussed earlier. Get to know as much about the people you meet as you can.

Get to know the security staff on a cruise ship. Feel free to talk to them and ask them what you should be mindful of. They may be able to give you tips on what to be careful of and most likely they'll be happy to help you. When things become popular as cruise ships have, it also becomes more popular with the criminal element. Cruise ship companies seem too guarded in releasing their crime statistics to suit my taste. The federal government is looking into the industry to better safeguard the millions of us who use this great vacation option. While becoming familiar and comfortable be somewhat guarded and prudent. I'm not saying to walk around with a frown on your face or the mindset of fear. After all, you're on vacation. Though, what I am saying is that you should again be aware and be a part of your security and ultimately your happiness.

Once you leave the ship and embark onto your visited ports, scams and thieves may be waiting to take advantage of you. Listen to your cruise-ship authorities who will tell you what to watch out for while visiting ports-of-call. Heed their advice.

While cruising along on beautiful ships is only a once in awhile activity for most of us, riding on trains or subways on the other hand are a daily necessity for many. When using subways, they can become extremely crowded which in turn can bring you into close contact with men. Some of these men may use this opportunity to "cop a feel" or in plain words touch you when and where you don't want to be touched. If that happens you can make a fuss and point or stare at the man while you chastise him in a loud voice. Make a scene; don't take that kind of behavior! On the flip side, try not to use empty cars if possible, again using the safety-in numbers technique. At night you may want to sit closer to the conductor or try to sit in a crowded car.

Also, it is safest not to sit in the first or last cars in case of a collision. If you happen to notice someone leave something on board and then leaving the train, use your instincts as whether to tell the conductor or not. In today's time many of us have concerns about the possibility of terrorists leaving explosives or chemical or biological agents in public places. By telling someone in authority it puts any further actions that may be appropriate in his trained "hands." The same goes for any suspicious person that you may see. Some subway riders may say that pretty much everyone they see on some rides seem suspicious. Well, I'm not going to argue with that one, but in such a case someone *really* suspicious, then. I mean someone that stands out from the usual suspicious types. Rely on your instincts to help you.

4

THE WORKPLACE, the surprising area of danger and how to deal with it

The work environment can at times be a place of concern for women. A woman who works for a large international company was getting into her car after work, in the company parking lot. When she sat down behind the wheel, she noticed a man hiding in the back seat waiting for her. The man was a co-worker whom she hardly even knew but whom apparently had a "crush" on her and she was able to talk him out of her car.

How brazen to sneak into a woman's car, hide in the backseat and I guess try to get what he fancied. Thankfully, this worked out well for the woman and was just one incident of concern occurring at the workplace.

A Surprising Area of Violence

Some fascinating facts regarding workplace violence show us that work, for many, is an unsafe place.

- Women are the victims in three-fifths of all reported incidents of workplace violence.
- Homicide is the leading cause of death among women in the workplace.
- In recent years, one out of four employees was harassed, threatened, or attacked in the workplace.
- Two out of three employees don't feel secure at work.
- Annual estimates for violent workplace incidents are as high as 2 million per year.

The types of workplace violence are:

- Threats

- Harassment
- Physical assaults
- Verbal abuse
- Sexual abuse
- Stalking

The perpetrators of workplace violence against women are:

- Employees
- Former employees
- Customers, clients or patients
- Family members or strangers passing by
- Outside acquaintances of employees

Some of the major reasons workplace violence occurs are:

- Work-related conflict
- Domestic violence that spills over to work
- A stalkers' obsession
- Personal conflict
- Robbery
- Sexual power-type issues (Rape and sexual assault)

Management must rise to the occasion to combat workplace violence. Not only because it's the right thing to do but also because employees have the legal right to be safe in the workplace. If companies do not address valid security concerns they're going to lose millions. A sound, comfortable work atmosphere is a productive atmosphere and a productive atmosphere is a profitable one. Smart companies will do what they can for their most important resource, their employees.

As for the incident mentioned at the beginning of this chapter about the woman who got into her car and found an unknown co-worker in the backseat, remember the best defense against that type of incident is to *always lock those car doors and look before you get in.* This goes for shopping, dining or wherever.

Remember, women have unique challenges facing them and sometimes a *little extra observation is in order.*

Don't get overly friendly with certain individuals who may seem "funny," unusual, weird or suspicious. Be pleasant and business-like but that's all. One of the worst types of people you can get involved with is a "stalker type" individual. This is someone who fixates on you and will not let go. Present psychological thinking is that there is no real cure for these people…no real way to get them away from you, no real psychotherapy that works. Recent laws give people more protection from these individuals, but even incarceration sometimes does not deter them from coming after you once they are released. *Keep away from people who seem too controlling or seem unusually shy or strange.*

Take your time getting to know the men you want to associate with at work or socially. Do not give your phone number out too freely and again be aware of your surroundings. Trust your cautious self.

All About Stalking

A report by the United States Department of Justice stated that 8.1% of women reported being stalked in their lifetime. If you feel you're in any possible phase of being stalked remember theses tips:

- Notify the police; keep them in the loop and ask for any and all assistance.

- Tell the stalker no, once and only once. The more you actually respond to him; in any way, the more you are communicating with him. Any more of a response may reinforce the stalking.

- Carry a cell phone with you everywhere you go.

- Never be afraid to sound your horn to attract attention.

- Do not accept any packages unless you ordered them or you were expecting them from friends or family members.

- Document; log everything having to do with your harasser or stalker. Keep letters and voice mail recordings.

- If you feel you are being followed do not drive home or to family or friends where the stalker could find out where you and yours live. Drive to a police station if at all possible.

- Take your name off of mailboxes or reserved parking areas.

- Have co-workers screen all your calls and visitors.

- Consider buying a dog or an alarm system.

- You can utilize a restraining order against a stalker. However restraining orders may actually incite a stalker to act out violently. Get advice from the police, a prosecutor or other experts on the best course of action in your particular case.

- Join a stalking victims' support group. Go on line to find one near you. They can give you detailed ways to block easy access to your address and other detailed and experienced tips.

Stalking is a problem for which there may be no easy answers or solutions. If you are affected it may require you to make significant changes in your life or lifestyle in order to be safe. Remember to utilize the experts from your local authorities and the support groups that are there to help you.

5

Dating and Socializing

While I'm not a dating expert and probably couldn't get a job as a social director, I certainly can help you in understanding some of the challenges women face when pursuing what they should, dating and socializing. I'm a person, who has seen what can happen to women who date the "wrong" type of person or frequent the wrong type of places. Date rapes, stalking activity and assaults can all occur to women when they hook up with the wrong type of person or if they frequent the wrong type of places.

Some "experts" in women's security say that to limit women as to their activities or even to a lesser degree in limiting what type of men they should date is wrong, limiting and sexist. Nonsense. Prudent people limit themselves everyday. I know a man that was a SWAT team police officer for a major metropolitan department for over ten years. He was big, strong and looked imposing and scary, certainly not a man that most in their right mind (or even not in their right mind) would attack or even bother. He was one of those men, kind of one in a million that you really would not want to mess with. Further, he had seen pretty much of everything from brawls, drug raids, shoot-outs to killings.

He told me that he knew of a very popular entertainment area that thousands frequented weekly, mostly at night, that he only went to during the day when it was apt to be safe. The popular area had started having trouble with some assaults and brawling. He was a man that enjoyed socializing and having a good time. However, he too, limited himself from going to the area other than when the chances were that it would be "safe". He told me that he didn't want to go to an area that he might have to fight, shoot or defend himself if he didn't have to. He limited himself, *as prudent, intelligent men and women do all the time.*

Probably the most important thing that I suggest for women in the dating world is to get to know the man you would like to go out with. Now that's Earth shattering advice, huh? It sounds so simple and sophomoric and it is something everybody wants to do anyway. Actually, what I am really suggesting is to go out of your way to *REALLY* get to know the man.

I am not suggesting going out and hiring a private detective to investigate everyone you plan on dating. What I am saying is to take a little longer period of extra time to observe him. If you work together, observe him there. Not only in how good looking, cool or charming he may be but also in what his real character is like. How does he handle stress or anger? Does he flip out over stress or when his anger is stirred up? We all get angry but some people take it too far or are brought to anger too easily. Do you want to risk him flying off the handle when you do or say something he doesn't like or when you tell him no? Does he truly care for people and enjoy life? Or does he just put on an act like he's so, so nice, just to impress. *Does he respect women and their opinions?* This is an important one for you to see in a man. *A man who truly respects women will not attempt a date rape. When a woman says no, he knows she means no, and he respects it.*

Don't be afraid to ask questions about a perspective suitor. It is your life and there is nothing wrong with taking an active role in its success. Take your time and use tact in your observations.

I realize that sometimes it's hard to take extra time to watch for these things. However, it can save you not only the obvious emotional trauma but also physical trauma. If you really cannot observe the man, try to go out with another couple, or meet him in a crowded area for your first or second get-together. Let friends and family know who you are going out with and where and what time you plan on getting home.

Be mindful of too much alcohol consumption by your date, and also by you. If you feel uncomfortable while you're out together, leave him or stay at the restaurant, bar or theater without him. You can find a way home if need be.

To be safe in the dating world, taking your time is the key phrase. You do not have to jump right in, right away. Usually the extra time and effort to get to know the man will not hinder your relationship with him at all. Wait for when the time is right and you're relatively sure the guy is stable and respectful. Sometimes it takes time but there are oodles of respectful men out there, some of them waiting for you.

DATE RAPE DRUGS

Unscrupulous people putting drugs into women's beverages are another dangerous act women have been subjected to. So much of it has occurred and continues to occur that the drugs used have a generic name called date-rape drugs.

In 1998 the maker of the drug Rohypnol which has been called the date-rape drug of choice made some changes to make them harder to misuse. The drug is now blue in color, will fizz when in liquid and most importantly will float at the top of a drink for about twenty minutes.

The problem with date-rape drugs is that a lot of different ones can be used by someone. Xanax-type drugs can and have been used and even LSD has been utilized. There are a lot of drugs that can make a woman lose control of herself. So be aware of your surroundings *by not leaving your drink unattended and watching as your drinks are being served to you.*

Not long ago a woman went to a party at a professional athlete's home late after the bars all closed down. The party started off with a fair amount of people drinking and dancing. According to the woman, pretty much the next thing she remembered was waking up in the morning in an empty bed with no pants on. She believed that she was given some sort of drug for someone to take advantage of her.

I don't know what the truth is in regards to this particular and ongoing case, but the fact of the matter is that people will use drugs to take advantage of women. They did it in the past and will do so in the future. Be careful.

Thinking Twice May Be the Key that Saves Your Life

On the subject of being careful, I know a man who teaches self-defense who used to be a bodyguard to high profile clients in business and Hollywood. Here is a man who is in great shape, knows how to fight, has had to use his skills protecting others and generally has been around the block and then some. So, guess how he feels about being careful? He just doesn't go to bars or to places where the chances are good for problems. He's careful, prudent and knowledgeable. He knows *there are places that are trouble, not fun, but trouble.* It's not that he never goes to a bar but he doesn't frequent any place that has a fairly high percentage of having trouble.

So, slow down and use your discerning self to think before you go out to a certain bar, nightclub or party.

- Ask yourself will you be there real late?
- Will you be with friends that will look out for you?
- Do you really know the people that are hosting a late-night after-bars-closed party?

Don't feel that you have to go to a bar or party when you know its bad news because you feel desperate in finding someone for you; you're better than that. No matter who you are, you are better than doing that to yourself and there are better places for you to find the one that will work out for you.

I have seen so many tears from women who wanted to be free spirits who could do whatever they wanted, wherever and whatever time they wanted to do it; because they thought that it would be fulfilling. I'm all for fulfilling but there are some basic facts that you have to watch out for.

- There are certain bars, nightclubs, parties and people you don't want to get near.

- There are users and abusers out there that look at you as nothing more than entertainment for them. Besides, quite often their entertainment isn't your idea of entertainment.

- There are places and people you as a smart woman, should stay away from, period.

Love Online

Everyday more and more people are getting into the on-line dating or meeting people world. Why not? The Internet is a fantastic resource in so many areas, why not in getting to know others? Some people have found excitement, relationships and even marriages on line. They also have found lies, deceit, assault, and abuse.

Until you find out for sure that the other person is genuine, you really have no idea whether he is violent, might stalk you or force you into sex *if given the opportunity.*

Here are some tips that you should consider if you plan on trying the Internet for dating and romance.

- Take your time and think carefully before you give out personal information such as your last name, phone number, address and place of work. If he pressures you to give the information up too quickly, stop communicating with him. Giving your home phone number to a man can make it extremely easy for him to find your home address (less than thirty seconds) simply by using a home computer.

- Remember he may not be who or what he says. Trust your instincts; leave the conversation when you are uncomfortable.

- Do not use your regular email address, set up another address for communicating with potential on line romances. If you plan on using your own email, make sure your email signature file is turned off or do whatever you need to do to make sure it does not show identifying information. Talk to your Internet Provider Service (IPS) in helping you keep this information away from potential "players."

- Use a phone to contact each other. A phone conversation can provide valuable information into a person's communication and social skills. You can make the call from a cell or pay phone.

- Take all the time you need to test for a trustworthy man. Look for inconsistencies.

- Only meet the man when you're absolutely ready.

Some warning signs that should keep you away:

- Disrespectful comments.

- Demeaning comments.

- Inconsistent information about personality characteristics.

- Does not want to talk to you on the phone after you have established an online relationship.

- Sounds too good to be true; he probably is.

- If he refers to a lot of Internet romance experiences, be cautious and put your guard up a little higher.

When you meet the man:

- Never arrange to have him pick you up at your home.

- Use your own transportation and choose a location where many people are present. Coffee houses and restaurants are good places.

- Consider taking a friend with you.

- If you go alone, tell a friend the man's name and phone number, location of the date, and also the time you plan on getting home.

- Trust your gut instinct and leave <u>anytime</u> you want to.

Certainty is not a term we often use in safety and security. Why, because nothing in security or self-defense is certain to work all of the time, every time, for everyone.

My example earlier about entering into fires too haphazardly was an action I had to adjust because it simply was not the right thing to do for my safety and security. When looking for romance on the Internet make sure you're cautious, you take your time and *stop going any further* when someone makes you uncomfortable.

Consider utilizing as many of the tips mentioned above as you can. Using these keys for Internet safety will not make it a certainty in keeping you completely safe, but it surely will make it more likely you'll have a pleasant and safe experience.

Anytime you're dealing with people that are anonymous and far away (out of human contact) your perceptions of face-to-face gut instincts are not as strong as if you really knew them from work, parties or social events. Remember that really knowing the truth about a man is harder, your well-being is more at risk and it's just plainly more difficult finding Mr. Right via the Internet. Bring your level of awareness up a notch or two and make sure you're cautious!

6

Rape and Sexual Assault

Sexual assault has got to be the biggest fear women have. It has occurred since the dawn of time. Years ago, and for that matter, to this day, during times of war when a faction or side overtook or overtakes an area or country, quite often women were and are raped. Throughout history during these times mothers would hide their daughters and women would try to stay out of the way of the conquering troops. During the 1991 attack and subsequent occupation of the Middle Eastern country Kuwait by its neighbor, Iraq, 100,000 women were reportedly raped.

Rape is almost never a sexual act; it is an act of power. Whatever the real reason behind rape is, it ends up as an abuse of a person that can have obvious immediate consequences. One of these consequences is, of course, a sexual assault along with the lasting psychological possibility of an unwanted pregnancy and venereal disease. Also, of course sexual assault can lead to the ultimate consequence of death.

Rape can be an extremely violent act, and I emphasize the word *extremely*. It can be and quite often is an act where a great deal of violence from punching, kicking and biting can occur…not just holding down and raping.

There was a case a few years ago where a rape was somehow videotaped and eventually used against the perpetrator to convict him. The tape showed such a level of violence against the woman that it was just about unbelievable. It showed the man repeatedly hitting the woman in the face so hard that you could hear thuds, as if he were hitting a melon. He kept hitting her as though she was a punching bag and about as hard as I've seen one person hit another. All the while he was telling her to do exactly what he wanted and when and how he wanted it done.

Some of the jurors who convicted the rapist were interviewed after their verdict. One man on the jury said that he wanted to literally leave the jury box while he was viewing the tape and beat the defendant up. That's how enraged he was by what he had seen. It was a terrible violent abuse of the woman. It took the jury a short time to convict this lowest form of predator. The man was convicted in near record time.

However, the big question is what do you do to not be raped? Well of course the things discussed earlier all come into play: being aware, knowing whom you are dealing with, carrying yourself a certain way, walking with others when possible, etc.

Quite often women who are raped know the person who rapes them. It is usually not some perfect stranger. This tells us again to be aware of who is around you. From the strange guy who may live in your apartment complex to the guy you may work with, be somewhat guarded and aware of who is in your sphere of life…as a woman you must.

Back off and report a person who invades your space more than once or twice or seems to gawk at you regularly. *If you can articulate certain actions that concern you as a woman, think seriously about reporting them.* Do not take any nonsense from a strange or concerning guy. Do not play mental games with anyone if they appear to be throwing them toward you. Be aware, be aware, and be aware! Do not be afraid to be firm and aloof with anyone who concerns you.

WHAT TO DO?…FIGHT, FLIGHT OR BETTER YET ANYTHING AND EVERYTHING!

What should a woman do when actually confronted with a sexual assault? Should you fight or just be submissive?

There are weapons that can be used if available. Except for now if you have nothing else to fall back on other than yourself, should you use fight, flight or just let it happen?

Of course, flight or getting away is always your best option if at all possible. As an example, if you are walking on a street and you notice a car following you, you can immediately turn and walk the opposite way. It's difficult for a car to just drastically turn and go the wrong way on a public roadway to keep following you.

Do Not Get in an Attackers Car

To lessen the chance of being kidnapped or raped, do not get into an attacker's car if he pulls out a gun and orders you to get in. Most attackers don't want to shoot you; they want to have their way with you first. Run away screaming! He can look for an easier target, not you. The best way short of being sheltered by appropriate cover to keep from being shot is movement. It is hard to hit a moving target even for the most accomplished shooter and the odds are the average gun-toting predator is not a gun expert. *Erratic, unpredictable movement is best but movement, any movement is a great defense from being shot.*

Whatever Works For You

Except what if a tactical move or an out and out flight does not work? What is the best thing to? Well, you should use everything you can to get away from being molested. That also may mean lying to the predator. Possibly trying to keep him away or off of you by telling him that you are ill with cancer or AIDS is an example. This has worked and will work again one day, I'm sure.

I have heard some rape experts say that this is not likely to work. I personally know of a situation where convincing two attackers that the victim was riddled with cancer worked to the point of them not going through with a sexual assault. They believed her convincing lie. It worked for her but will it work on another predator? Well yes and no. To some I suppose it would work and on others, no way. Although, this woman tried it and it worked. She read the situation correctly. She was robbed but not raped. She had a scar on her body that she used to her advantage. She convinced them that the scar was related to her body being full of cancer. She thought on her feet. *She used what was available, prudent and workable at that particular time and for that specific situation.*

For you it may be another lie or *thing* that may work for your situation. Think on your feet. Think…how in the world can I survive this? How can I stop this from happening? Your wits may rise to the occasion. Some examples of women that thought on their feet:

- A woman was leaving a nightclub one evening and decided to walk alone to her car. She was trained in Martial Arts and as she walked up to a deserted looking building a man jumped out from the shadows and started running at her. She turned her body to the side a little and kicked him with a "side kick" (a basic, cornerstone martial art kick) in his stomach area. The man fell backwards almost all the way to the ground and ran away.

- A woman was leaving a party one evening and decided to take a path in the woods that led to her parked car. She had about 8 years of martial arts training and felt calm as she walked. As she was walking on the desolate path a man jumped out from behind a tree and grabbed her from behind in a bear-hug. She tried some of her martial arts moves against the man but they did not work. She was going to try another move, a head-butt on the assailant, but just before she was going to try it, he pulled a knife and held it tightly to her throat. She stopped fighting and eventually was raped. After the ordeal she said she felt if she had continued to fight, he would have killed her. She further went on to say she felt her martial arts training enabled her to remain calm and also assess the situation, which for her was to stop fighting. By doing so, she felt she would survive to live another day.

- A man grabbed a woman from behind one night as she walked alone. He had her in a bear-hug type hold. The woman had some self-defense train-ing and she immediately stomped down hard on the person's foot, whereas he let her go and ran away.

All of these women thought on their feet. They also all happened to have some self-defense or martial art training and they all tried to actively and physically get away from their attackers. For two of them, the quick, hard and correct moves for *their* particular circumstance worked. For another it didn't. Or didn't it? She felt that she should stop fighting, that it was the best thing she could do for herself. I for one will not argue with her decision. Thinking on our feet means quickly assessing the *correct thing to do at the correct time, for our particular situation.*

However, all of these women did do something wrong. What was it? It was that they walked alone at night and in some cases in secluded areas. This is the wrong thing to do unless it's the *only* thing you can do. Do not walk alone on dark wooded desolate paths if you don't have to. Walk with others at night if you can and especially in desolate or people-free areas.

Some stories of women that either didn't have or didn't rely on any formally taught physical self-defense moves are:

- A woman told police that after coming home one night she was attacked by an intruder inside of her home. She said she bit his hand and he ran from the apartment.

- One night a woman was approached by a man who looked her straight in the eye and said hey..."I'd like to have sex with you." The woman promptly replied, "You'd better stay away because the police are looking for me. I've just killed my husband." He left, quickly.

- The Chicago Sun-Tribune reported that on May of 2001 a 42 year old woman told police that she fought back after a man forced her to perform oral sex on him. Police put two testicles in a biohazard evidence container. Not too long afterwards a man turned up at a hospital minus, yes, you guessed it, his testicles. While doctors attempted to re-attach them, the police charged him with aggravated criminal sexual assault.

Before I go on, realize it may get to the point that a lie, an excuse, a threat or fighting to the best of your ability just does not work (similarly to the wooded path incident). You fail, you are vanquished, you are sexually assaulted, or you are raped. Although, the chances are that you will survive. Furthermore, as you do survive, you will make it. You will get the help that is available by the tons of caring people and organizations that are accessible and willing to assist. *You will go on and flourish, remember this. This is not just a pep talk for you. It's true. You can make it.*

The Question of Whether to Fight

Getting physical or fighting should be done when you feel that it's the thing to do. Sounds like a cop-out, doesn't it? I don't mean it to be, but if you feel that it will work, that it's what you want to do, and you feel it's the best thing to do in your circumstance, then do it. Do it hard. Do not stop. Do not hesitate. Go for broke, as I like to say, in other words take that plunge. In a nutshell what I'm saying is doing the right workable thing or things for a given circumstance.

Some statistics show that over 50% of victims that took self-protective measures felt it helped their situation. Wow, *this is telling us that if you do take self-protective action, you may very well have a 50% chance of helping yourself.*

Should I know how to fight then, you may ask? Or should I just do what kind of comes naturally like kicking, biting and punching? The best thing of course is to know what to do; to have the most amounts of training and knowledge you can gather. If that's not possible for your circumstances, less training is acceptable and might work for you. Some experts say to run, fight and yell as loud as possible if you are attacked. This option is sound advice for anyone being attacked.

If you have never really been trained but possibly you have read a little about survival or maybe you've taken one of those short self-defense classes, even then you could win and survive. Or maybe your awareness is not the greatest and you really do not have any fighting experience. Nonetheless, you're motivated, let me repeat you are MOTIVATED to bite, kick, punch or pick up a pencil and shove it in the bad guy's head. If you're properly motivated to survive, that too can work. It's up to each of you to do what you feel is the right thing to do in that particular moment.

The statistics gathered below are from a study done in the 1990's. It's about what happened when victims attempted self-protective measures during times of rape or sexual assault.

Rape/sexual assault victims	485,290
Victim took self-protective action	71.7%
Victim took no self protective action	28.3%
Resisted or captured offender	19.3%
Scared or warned offender	11.5%
Persuaded or appeased offender	10.8%
Ran away or hid	6.9%
Attacked offender without weapon	6.1%
Screamed from pain or fear	3.7%
Got help or gave alarm	3.6%
Other measures	9.8%

It's interesting to note that there were many different tactics or measures victims tried and used.

Among the victims who took self-protective action, a little over half said that their actions helped the situation. About 1 in 5 victims felt that their actions either made the situation worse or simultaneously helped and worsened the situation.

Some further statistics are listed below to shed a little factual light on sexual assault. Between 1993 and 2001 rape and sexual assaults had gone down over 50% percent. Great news but don't forget, trends change. A study reported by the *Rape Abuse and Incest Network* (RAINN) states that in 2001 there were 249,000 victims of rape, attempted rape and sexual assault in the United States. Of this number eighty-four thousand were victims of completed rapes.

- 15% of victims were under the age of twelve.
- 29% percent were age twelve-seventeen.
- 44% were under the age of eighteen.
- 80% were under the age of thirty.
- The average age of an arrested rapist was thirty-one.
- In 2001 about 7% of rapes involved the use of a weapon.

- About four out of ten sexual assaults take place at the victim's home.
- Two in ten took place in the home of a friend. One in ten took place outside, away from home.
- About one in twelve took place in a parking garage.

Some more generalized statistics show that:

- 43% of rapes occur between 6p.m. and midnight.
- 24% percent occur between midnight and 6a.m.
- 33% take place between 6a.m. and 6p.m.
- 66% of rape victims know their assailant.
- Approximately 48% of victims are raped by a friend or acquaintance.
- 30% are raped by a stranger.
- 16% percent are raped by an intimate.

In the next year, 2002, 247,730 rapes, attempted rapes and sexual assaults were reported almost mirroring 2001's numbers.

Statistics can be a helpful tool if we look at them for our particular needs. Access these statistics and find the areas you may not have been familiar with or that may help you deal positively with the way you live your life presently.

7

Tools To Protect Women, all the way from toasters to handguns, it's your choice

There are tools that people all across the world use to protect themselves. Tools used in this context means items that help people protect themselves. People have been using them since the beginning of time.

Probably one of the oldest tools used by man is still being used in an organized manner today by police agencies across the world. It is the club, or as we now call them a nightstick or a baton. The modern police straight baton is the impact weapon of choice throughout the world for most police agencies. There have been variations to the straight baton throughout time but the variations were similar in their original function as an impact weapon.

A stick kind of weapon that hurts when you get smacked by it or worse yet causes damage to the person getting hit. Essentially this weapon has stayed the same since the beginning of time.

The point is that men and women have has been using items to protect themselves forever. While the baton or a "big stick" is a useful tool for police it is however, not the tool or weapon of choice for the average person trying to protect themselves. Could you imagine walking around with a baton or a big stick? Or how about walking into work and propping your stick on your desk while you did your work, then walking to your car with it? People would think you're a real loony tune. Come to think of it though, you probably wouldn't be messed with by anyone. I'm just kidding, it's not recommended.

Probably the first tool man used to protect himself was the rock. It was available and it was hard. When we're confronted to the point that we need to protect ourselves there are many things available. Rocks, knives, lamps, toasters, sticks, pens, pencils, keys, pots, pans and really *anything that will hurt or cause the bad guy damage can be used.*

Key's or pencil's can be used to jab someone in areas such as the:

- Jaw
- Temple
- Throat
- Eyes
- Ribs
- Stomach

Pots, pans, rocks, toasters and the like can be used as impact weapons focusing on areas such as the:

- Head
- Back
- Arms
- Knees
- Legs
- Hands

A big key when using a weapon is to use it with *bad intentions*. You cannot lightly strike someone unless you are trained in a particular weapon and you can really gauge your striking power in response to your threat. The average untrained woman who is going to use a weapon must go for it with great fervor to cause damage and inflict pain. It is not pretty and it's not nice. You definitely don't want to strike someone lightly and just get him or her angrier. *If you are going to hit someone, if you get to that point, be serious.* Go for it.

Think of this gruesome analogy. Imagine holding an apple in your weaker hand. With your free hand use your index finger and poke the apple. Go ahead and poke it. Apples are pretty hard and a normal kind of poke if there is such a thing, will dent it, bruise it and maybe even tear it. Now, keep imagining...now poke that apple with every ounce of strength you can muster into that index finger. While you're poking, do not consider or even care that it might hurt or even break your finger. You're poking as fast, as hard and with as much bad intention as you can muster. Poke it. Now look at that apple. It has a hole in it, a deep hole. Now imagine that apple being the eye of a Ted Bundy or some other twisted person trying to harm you. An eyeball is not as hard as an apple, so think...what can you do to an eye? It's gross and hopefully you will never have to resort to doing it on an eye, but that's how "going for it" works.

As technology has progressed throughout the years, protection tools or weapons have also progressed. There are a number of self-protection weapons out there. The most dramatic and familiar is the firearm. It also is the most controversial.

Years ago in the old western days the Colt handgun was said to be the great equalizer for man. There was a saying that God did not create man equal, Sam Colt, the founder of the Colt firearm, did. Possibly cold and not politically correct today, but true in the context mentioned.

There has been a great deal of controversy concerning firearms in our country and across the world. Not wanting to get into the hullabaloo swelling about the subject I will say that it is the ultimate available personal self-defense weapon. This is a fact that cannot be disputed.

A firearm is better than a club, a knife or whatever. If cavemen had access to firearms in their time you can bet they would have used them instead of the club. Saying this, it must also be said it is an unforgiving weapon. This is to say that it takes continuous practice to stay safe and proficient with a firearm and more specifically, a handgun. A mistake with a handgun can be a major tragedy that cannot be fixed, changed or made right. If a person makes a mistake with a handgun it can be disastrous.

A mistake with it can maim, blind, cripple, disfigure or kill an innocent person. Safety in its use and storage is paramount and must be followed.

Carrying a concealed handgun used to be illegal in most states. Now, many states however, allow people to carry concealed pistols with an approved permit. More and more states are following this trend of issuing licenses. As of the beginning of 2005, 46 states allowed its citizenry to get concealed handgun permits.

Across the country there also has been a big upsurge of women buying handguns for protection. They do not necessarily buy them to carry them but quite often for home protection. Also in my opinion, they are the best home protection weapons. However, and this is a big *however*, if one is to make the choice of using a firearm for home protection, many things must be considered and done.

The first thing, all legal requirements should be followed. Check with your state and local authorities for guidelines. Second, proper training is a must before any use of a firearm is contemplated. This is to say, before you get ready for self-protection use, you should get competent training. Then, after initial training, practice should be continuous. For instance, you can join a gun club that specifically trains and practices on a regular basis. You must become familiar and then *stay* familiar with the safe and proper use of the weapon. You must follow the proper ways to store the firearm at home. The three fundamental gun safety rules are:

- Always keep the gun pointed in a safe direction.
- Always keep your finger off the trigger until ready to shoot.
- Always keep the gun unloaded until ready to use.

Some other important basic rules are:

- Be sure the gun is safe to operate.
- Know how to use the gun safely, read the manual, and get competent training.
- Use only the correct ammunition for the gun.
- Store guns and ammunition so they are not accessible to unauthorized persons including children.

You must keep up with this dangerous yet unmistakably effective weapon. A firearm is a major commitment that has to be taken seriously. It is a commitment that I suspect many people cannot or will not make. Well, that's fine. They are not for everyone.

The next highly effective self-protection tool is pepper spray. It's called pepper spray because it is actually made from pepper. I believe it was originally made to protect outdoorsmen from bears. Guides outfit many outdoorsmen to this day with pepper spray before they go out into bear country. Wow, something that will work against a bear must be some good stuff! It is, but like anything, it's not perfect or one hundred percent.

Pepper spray comes in different forms. It comes in an aerosol type canister where the pressing of a button shoots the effective pepper ingredient out. It comes out in either a:

- Stream
- Strong cone-shaped mist
- Fog, (wide type blast)
- Foam, that sticks to what it hits

The stream spray is the most accurate and works the best in windy conditions because it shoots out as a straight pressurized stream. However, it is not the most effective. The cone-shaped sprays along with the fogger type units have particles that stay in the air, which in turn enters the attacker's lungs and causes more distress.

The foam has the least cross contamination and is very effective. By cross contamination I mean that when pepper spray is used let's say in a house, not only the person who is hit by the spray is affected, but others caught by a residual mist that remains in the general area, experience the effects to a lesser degree. However, when you're using it to protect yourself or your loved ones, cross contamination is not your main concern. It is, however, a concern.

I have been in areas where people have been sprayed and the residual amount that I breathed in affected me pretty badly. I had great difficulty breathing and had to continuously get fresh air to function well. Again, these were times I was not directly sprayed but I was in the enclosed room where someone else had been sprayed. It makes people who are sprayed cough, have difficulty breathing and makes it extremely difficult for a person to see. It also burns like crazy and really hurts the person sprayed.

Because of the possible cross contamination that may occur with certain types of sprays I recommend the foam-type spray. I have been told by people who have been sprayed by it, that it not only involuntarily made their eyes shut and made it difficult to breathe, but that it just plain HURT, terribly.

The foam type pepper spray comes out similar to the straight stream spray and is accurate. Pepper spray affects people differently. Some of the reasons that contribute to the differences are:

- Did the spray get to his face well or just barely?
- Was the person sprayed for a long enough period?
- Was the brand of spray a quality product? I was filming a training video for policemen when an officer helping in the taping caught a slight bit of spray, from the quality brand we were using. He coughed and had difficulty breathing. Whereas, about a year before he actually was sprayed directly in the face with another brand of spray that hardly affected him at all.

I have used pepper spray many times and it has been effective. I'm also aware of times that it was used on out of control violent people where it has been effective, however, to a lesser degree. The points listed below I suspect might have been the cause or causes of the less than expected results.

- The lack of a quality brand product.
- Not spraying directly into the face.
- Not getting enough of the spray into the face.
- Possibly spraying from too close (less than about 2 feet).

However, nothing is perfect, not even firearms for that matter, and different people handle things differently.

I recently read an article written by a police officer who was relating his negative opinion on the use of pepper spray for self-defense. He felt that you could still function after being sprayed and it was not a good choice for self-defense purposes. He explained that as part of his department's training he would get sprayed each year by a pepper spray product and still perform certain police-related tasks such as shooting. The thinking behind this type of training is to get officers as familiar and as experienced as possible with the possibility of someone using pepper spray against them. His thinking was that if he could still perform these important functions, a bad guy could also. While I commend his department's realistic training (many departments have been doing this for years) he is incorrect in his assumption of pepper spray being a poor tool for self-defense.

An incident an officer told me about shows an example of the realities and importantly the limitations of weapons. The officer was patrolling one afternoon when he noticed a car pull into a gas station in front of him. The way he pulled into the station and the look on the driver's face made the officer think he might have been lost and in need of some directions. The policeman, who happened to be a K-9 officer, got out of his cruiser and approached the driver. When he got up to the car the driver immediately became agitated and asked him why he was being stopped. The officer told the man he was not stopping him and pointed out that he didn't have his overhead flashing lights on. The man stepped out of his car and the two started talking.

By now the officer was concerned. He had followed sound police procedure and given the license plate number of the car to his dispatcher before he got out of his cruiser.

While he was talking to the man he heard radio traffic come over his portable radio that the car he was out with had just been involved in an armed robbery. The officer told me the man started bringing his hand toward him quickly and he thought he was going to be stabbed or shot but instead the man punched him in the face.

When he was hit, his K-9, a German Shepherd, bolted out of the cruiser and attacked the man. The guy quickly pulled a knife and started stabbing the dog. The dog continued his attack even as the man was stabbing him. Remember, this is all happening quickly. Finally, the dog collapsed and could no longer protect his partner. The man, knife in hand, started walking at the officer, who told him to stop. The man kept coming at him and the officer aimed at the center of his body mass and fired two shots from his 357-magnum revolver. The officer told me after he fired those shots he continued coming directly at him and he shot two more times, still aiming at his torso. The man did not even seem to flinch and just kept coming at the policeman. The workers in the gas station were watching this happening and were thinking to themselves that the officer's shots were missing the man.

The officer, still keeping an aim on the man, continued telling him to stop. The attacker growled something to the effect of "you killed my mother" and kept coming at him. The officer now aimed at his forehead and shot once, hitting and killing him instantly.

Later, they found that all of the officers rounds (four) hit in the center mass of the assailant, just where policeman are taught to shoot. Yet, the man kept on coming, so much so witnesses thought all the bullets were totally missing him.

Autopsy reports later showed no trace of alcohol or drugs in the assailant. The point is nothing is perfect and works all the time in the same way on everybody. In this case a large firearm did not stop the man for a long period of time. The officer kept his head, and actually accessed the situation as it progressed. By the way, the faithful German Shepherd lived through his ordeal and get this, chomped at the bit to get back to police work, which he did, returning to his beloved duties.

An example of pepper spray working well but taking time to be completely effective is the time I sprayed an individual who was big, crazed, and totally out of control. He told officers at the scene to go ahead and shoot him because he didn't care and he was ready to take us on. I sprayed him with a long blast and after about 10 seconds he was totally submissive and let us control him. He immediately reacted in our favor after being sprayed, but after about 10 or so seconds he was completely ours.

During the time leading up to pepper spray working at its optimum level, a person should do her best to keep out of an attacker's reach. In this particular case we did not stay out of his reach and we immediately grabbed him. It would have been better to *let the spray dig in and take strong effect.*

Some important keys to remember with pepper spray use are:

- The use of a quality product, (they are not created equal).

- A direct and as long as possible spray to the attackers face.

- This is critically important, keeping out of the assailant's grasp while spraying.

- Always be ready to retreat or advance to the rear if possible while spraying.

- Pepper spray is a good self-defense tool against an attacker attempting to harm you.

The problem with pepper spray or a handgun for that matter, is that if it's in your purse or deep in a coat pocket and it's not ready at hand immediately, it can be useless. I teach firearm basics, handling and safety for individuals who want to apply for concealed weapon permits in Ohio. They must complete this type of training before they can apply for a license through the state.

In one of our classes we had a responsible storeowner who was going to apply for a concealed weapon permit because there had been several store robberies and shootings near his business, one of which ended up in the murder of a young female store clerk. He told me that he was going to keep his handgun in his brief-case while he was at work, working the counter of his store. I told him unless he needed a paperweight in his briefcase not to put his gun there thinking it would be ready for his protection. Another instructor and I explained the ready at hand musts and different types of holsters he could use and yet have his firearm be totally concealed. If someone is to use these "tools" they must be *completely* at hand and ready to use. Be sure to remember this.

Police specialty stores that also sell to the public are good places to buy quality pepper spray products. Also, it would not be a bad idea to find someone who puts on a short training class for the general public in your area.

Is pepper spray legal? It's legal in all 50 states; however, there are some restrictions (as of this writing) in the following states.

- California—size limitations

- Massachusetts—size limitations and must have a "firearms Identification card"

- Michigan—Certain Michigan formula only

- New York—Limitations on where they must be purchased
- Wisconsin—Limitations on UV dyes

There may be new state or local regulations regarding pepper spray that aren't listed. Check with your local police department to make sure they are legal where you're living or if there are any restrictions.

Electrical Devices

A stun gun is a personal protection tool that has been around for at least 20 years. It is not to be mistaken for the Taser that is becoming very popular, lately. The stun gun is an instrument that is about the size of an electric razor (a little bit bigger). When activated it emits an electrical current that continues until you, the operator, turns it off. Policemen have used it in the past and some still do. I have only seen it used once on an unruly, intoxicated man. The man wasn't wearing a shirt and was resisting arrest when an officer put it to his bare chest and activated it. It had absolutely no noticeable effect on him.

This was many years ago and technology has changed for the better. Also, not everything works on everyone as I mentioned about the knife wielding man being shot by the officer. Although, another thing that concerns me about a stun gun is that you have to get right up to the assailant, touch him with it and then activate it. That's too close in my opinion. As an example with pepper spray you do *not want to get any closer than 2 feet to your target.* I do not recommend them for women's security.

Tasers

Tasers are electrical producing devices that look similar to that of a handgun. Many policemen carry them in a holster on their utility belts. They're differently colored, for example orange, to make it easy to differentiate them from guns. To use them, one aims the device at the assailant and shoots it very similarly to a gun. Electrical wires or prongs shoot out at the target carrying with it a high level of electricity. The prongs reach the assailant and the electricity incapacitates or greatly interferes with their ability to harm others.

I have never seen them used in the field. I have heard of instances where it had not worked well at all. The infamous Rodney King fiasco in Los Angeles, where a man was filmed being beaten with batons by police, was "Tasered" before the beating. Apparently, it didn't work well on him either. Again, not every thing works on everyone, and this very well may have been the case in the Rodney King case and others instances where they were not affective.

Also, and importantly, there are new updated versions of Tasers now servicing the police community that will soon be available to the general public for self-defense use. These new Tasers are said to be much better than the ones during the time of the Rodney King situation. These new Tasers used by police are said to be quite effective in handling unruly or dangerous people. In the same breath though, the Chicago Police Department as of February, 2005, has just suspended any and all use of Tasers for their officers when one man died and another teen-ager almost died after being "tasered". Other areas in the country have experienced similar concerns with the use of Tasers.

I do not recommend them at this point; I feel the jury is still out on this tool. However, the new generation Tasers seem to hold a lot of positive promise and may soon be an accepted, effective tool for the average man and woman.

Pens, pencils and keys can be effective weapons also. Many experts suggest women carry their keys in their hands walking to or from their cars, where they can be used quickly as a weapon, if need be. This is great advice. Think of the finger and apple example. A key, pen or pencil used against an attacker's temple as an example, can kill and most importantly for you, can stop the action against you.

Toasters and Telephones; Weapons?

Any solid, hard object like a telephone, toaster, vase, bottle, pot or pan can be effective weapons…not to mention sharp objects such as scissors or knives. With a weapon as with any self-defense strikes and moves, hesitation is a no-no. One must dive right in and use it quickly with power, speed and bad intentions. Going ahead tentatively will not work well, if at all. Use a weapon quick, hard and repeatedly, if necessary. Also, do not telegraph your weapon—this means use the pen, knife or hairbrush in a surprise move. Do not show him what you have in your hand or what you may have picked up. Let it be a surprise move on your part and then explode with speed, power and intensity when you use it against him.

An absolutely excellent weapon to have for those of you that walk for health or enjoyment purposes, or just walk a lot is the walking stick. Some people carry them to keep dogs away and they work great for that. Actually a walking stick can keep humans away also. Give it some thought…do you think a predator would likely go after a woman carrying a three foot stick? Probably not, and then if you add a confident, strong demeanor…what do you think?

The only time we use weapons are to defend ourselves from the possibility of being on the receiving end of serious physical harm or death. The law, generally speaking allows people to defend themselves using the amount of force necessary to stop the attack against them. This may be hard to gauge for the average person struggling to survive from a would-be attacker.

Pepper spray is a weapon that does not cause serious physical harm when it's used against someone. Again, pepper spray is not considered a deadly tool and yet works well.

So, the concern people may have with using a weapon such as a gun should not be there for the use of a pepper spray product.

As an example, using a key to strike someone in the temple can cause serious physical harm or death, as is the case with a firearm.

Some women may be fearful of using weapons to protect themselves, partly because of not knowing when *they* are really allowed to use them. While consulting a competent attorney is always the smart thing to do to understand the general rules in your locality on the use of force to protect yourself, the general rule of thumb is to use only the amount of force necessary to stop the force being used against you. That's a hard one to figure out for some.

When do you know that the guy coming at you snarling is going to do serious physical harm to you? How do you know that a person kicking in your door is going to kill you or do serious physical harm to you or loved ones? How do you know that a man that has grabbed you by the wrist and is pulling you toward a car or a dark area is going to do serious harm to you? Let's take a closer look at each scenario.

A Man Running at You

For instance, a man is running at you snarling (whatever that means) in a dark, secluded parking lot. The question is do *you* fear for yourself? Do you *sincerely fear* that this person may do serious physical harm to you? The answer is yes. The possibility of great bodily harm or death would be a concern for any woman alone in a dark, secluded area being charged at by a man, snarling or not.

If you had a firearm in this case and it was immediately ready at hand as it should be, *you may have the chance* to warn this man. This could be accomplished by pulling the gun out, pointing it at him and saying something like "Stop, I have a gun, do not come any closer." Talking to a person while you're using a weapon against him is always a good idea. As an example, statements such as "Stop, get away," "leave now," "get away and I'll stop spraying," and things of that nature are always good ideas. It can actually direct the man in your favor. It can give him the impetus to stop his attack, to listen to reason. Because, being faced with a weapon would make a reasonable or even a non-reasonable man seriously consider stopping his attack. By verbalizing, you can start and reinforce the process of stopping an attack against you.

If this same man, in the parking lot, got to you and started grabbing you, I would say again, that in my opinion, you reasonably would fear for your life or at the bare minimum the possibility of serious physical harm. So, if you had a key in your hand, I would say that sticking him with it anywhere would be prudent. This also means sticking it as many times necessary for him to let you go. Then when you can get away, go as fast as you can. Your goal really is not to hurt the man; it's to have him stop his attack. Hurt happens to go along with it. *You have the right to live and you have the right to use force if necessary.*

A Man kicking in Your Door

You and your child are at home alone one night and you hear someone kicking at your door trying to get inside. You immediately call 911 and tell the police what's going on. However, now the door's starting to give way and whoever is kicking at it is almost in. What do you do? Would a prudent or reasonable woman think that her life and the life of her child are at risk, or at least of being seriously physically harmed? You bet.

If you have a weapon, let's say a handgun, would it be prudent to shoot? In this particular case it certainly would be prudent to get your handgun and take your child to a safe room, such as your bedroom and lock the door. If at all possible staying on the line with the police is best, but after making that first 911 call your main priority is to keep you and your child safe. Once in the "safe-room," prepare to confront the intruder if he makes it into the house.

If he's inside and now trying to get into the bedroom, communicate with him. Tell him that you have a gun and you will shoot, tell him to leave. Keep telling him to get out, get away, that you have a gun and you will shoot him if he comes closer. If he breaks down the bedroom door and starts coming at you…shoot him. You've done smart, reasonable and prudent actions to survive. You had the time and ability to take these actions.

Sometimes, like in this scenario all may not be what it appears to be. I know of a case where an off-duty policeman was at home sleeping one night, when he was awakened by the loud sounds of someone trying to break down a door to his house.

He grabbed his gun and took cover near the door, where he could plainly hear someone in the act of pushing and breaking the door in. He hollered for the person to stop and leave. The person kept on kicking and pushing at the door. The homeowner continued hollering at him, telling him to leave and to get away. The person wouldn't stop and finally broke the door down and came into the house. The homeowner shot the man, stopping him from coming any further.

It turned out the man who broke the door down was the next door neighbor; in a drunken state he mistook his neighbor's house for his own. He apparently could not comprehend the commands to get away and stop.

The local county prosecutor reviewed the facts of the case and ruled that the shooting was justifiable. By the way, the neighbor lived and my guess is, probably quit drinking.

Pulling You in a Car, Against Your Will

If someone is pulling you in a car against your will of course you're in fear for your life or at least in fear that you will be seriously hurt and anything you can do to stop the man from kidnapping you is in order.

Your Attitude is the Key

Remember the key to using a weapon on someone is your attitude. The correct attitude is one of, using a weapon *because you must,* to survive and "make it". You do not want to use a weapon to be a mean person or to teach a nasty man a lesson. You don't want to use a weapon simply because you can, or that you have this "power in your hands". Your attitude in using a weapon is simply one of; a *necessity,* necessities that can help you continue with your good health and life. Approach the use of a weapon as an *acceptable* option that is available for you to survive.

8

Self-Defense When Being Attacked

Are taking self-defense courses a good thing for women? The answer is yes. They can truly make females have the ability to compete against a male attacker on a more even keel. But there are some definite things to consider and remember when a woman is going to get involved in self-defense training.

There are numerous types of training women can get involved in. My father has taught self-defense for most of his adult life. He's taught literally thousands of people throughout the years and continues to teach to this day. The style of martial art he teaches is called Minna Jiu-Jitsu that he invented about forty years ago. This style of self-defense combines Japanese Judo and Jiu-Jitsu with Korean Karate and French Foot Fighting, which is called Savate.

I personally became involved in the martial arts at about the age of eight. Not because I wanted to, but because I grew up in a martial arts family and I had to. As I got older I gained a different perspective and desire to stay involved in it on my own. I've also been involved in other styles of fighting arts throughout my life and have seen numerous types or styles of self-defense and tons of different instructors. I also have seen hundreds of students, many of whom would be in trouble if they'd get into a serious street survival fight.

It is so important to find the right style of self-defense, *one that deals with how to survive and how to do physical damage quickly and seriously to a person who is trying to do the same to you or your loved ones.* That is what self-defense boils down to.

Surviving in a life or death situation is serious, ugly stuff. As the old saying goes war is hell and that's what we are talking about here, personal warfare, and it *is* hell. It's not a philosophical discussion or a religious journey. It is serious business and getting involved in a style or with an instructor who really does not know the realities of self-defense, can give you a false sense of confidence that can have serious consequences for you.

There are many self-defense styles available throughout the country and for me to give my personal opinion on them would really not help you very much. *All different self-defense styles have their merits.*

Your Guide To Safety

First, look for an instructor who knows that defense training is a serious commitment, one that takes a long and continuous process of work and training *to be sharp, on target and very effective.* What you have to do while looking into defense training is to look for a school and instructors that teach realistic fight or rape training, and their instructors have the mindset of-realism training. Bruce Lee, probably the most famous martial art expert in modern history, said that he could not teach someone martial arts; he could only help the student discover things about her or himself. He could help in that personal discovery. *A good teacher helps you to help yourself.*

Some experts do not think that self-defense training has to be a long serious commitment. In a way I agree with them. You can take a short, well—structured self-defense course for women that can help you prevail in an attack. After all, women have prevailed without any formal training, and the fact of the matter is that some training is definitely better than no training whatsoever.

Whether one is to go the long route of serious commitment, or a shorter self-defense or rape defense course, it's still paramount that an instructor truly has that realism mindset and that a woman truly commits to the training given, no matter its length.

An Eye Opener For Taking Things Seriously

If you're going to get involved in self-defense training you should go all the way. Going half of the way can have bad consequences for you. What I mean is that when you take that "shorter class" or a long continuous training program, taught by a no-nonsense, realistic teacher, you must commit to it. Open your eyes and discern what the instructions mean for you *personally* and figure out how to make them work against a determined male thug.

In June of 2004 a security camera picked up a terrible assault that occurred in a pizza parlor in Akron, Ohio. What the camera captured was so vicious that not only did local media show it but CNN and Fox News showed it all across the nation. There were about 6 people at the counter. Some seemed to be placing orders while some were there to pick up their pizzas. One man took offense to a female that apparently cut in line to place her order. There was some cross words exchanged between the two. A store employee actually came out from behind the counter and confronted the woman at about the same time the camera showed her spiting at the employee. Right around this time, a large man, about 6'4" and about 290 pounds, came in. Apparently, the woman who was hollering, now at the employee and the man in line was either the girlfriend or at the very least a friend of the big guy.

The camera showed the big guy saying something to the man in line and then out of nowhere, sucker punching him. A sucker punch is hitting someone when they are not expecting it. One punch would have been enough for this big guy because the much smaller man looked to be in shock after the first punch. Though, he just kept winding up and letting go, punching him in the face, continually. None of the others in the shop did anything to help the man. Finally, the man collapsed to the floor.

The good news was that the police quickly caught the man. He was tried, convicted and very swiftly sentenced to 4 years in prison. The other man was seriously hurt.

I bring this example up for you to realize that there are big, not caring, violent people out there. Here was a man that none of the 3 or 4 other men in the shop wanted to get involved in, to help a man getting *pummeled*. This was a big, scary, violent man that when the put-up or shut-up time came, several good-sized men were apparently paralyzed with fear and didn't want to "mess" with him.

How about you, how would you react if a monster type animal like this man attacked you? Well…there are certain moves mentioned in the self-defense section of this book that can work enough for you to get away from a man such as this.

However, this example shows us that we must be serious and learn moves that really work. Not mumbo jumbo stuff that some experts say like; you as woman can kick someone in the groin or use your forearm to hit someone in the nose and you're going to be just fine. Yes, kicking in the groin may work and using a fist or a forearm may work also. However, some violent, crazed men are not pushovers and a kick to the groin or an un-trained punch to the nose is not going to do much.

An un-trained punch to the nose of the guy in this story wouldn't have done much. An averagely placed kick to the groin probably wouldn't have done much either. A finger shoved two inches into his eye socket would have. A well-placed eye gouge (that I show in the next chapter) very well may have worked enough for you to get away from a man similar to the man described above. There are things that can work for you, but do not leave your God given commonsense at the door when getting yourself ready to find a teacher or self-defense class. Take your safety seriously and make sure it's taught to you by someone that will help you understand the realities of what will really work.

A good teacher is one that can truthfully answer your questions about how your strike, kick, or gouge is apt to affect your assailant. Not everything will work for everyone. The instructor that you want in your corner will look at you as an individual with your certain musculature, reflex, speed and mind-set positives and liabilities and work and develop from there.

Becoming proficient, as a self-defense practitioner in the context that I'm talking about is more challenging for a female than a male. The biggest challenge to overcome or to develop for women in general is the lack of muscle strength compared to that of males. Proper, consistent training can develop a female in the direction to be able to compete successfully against a determined or enraged male attacker. This takes a lot of work, a great deal of determination and also the correct mental attitude. These can all be greatly enhanced by the right no nonsense, realistic instructor.

For a female to be able to defend herself against an enraged male attacker is difficult. It's not generally an easy prospect that can be taken lightly by a woman. It takes hard work and proper mental attitude. Women generally start with a distinct disadvantage that needs to be equalized as much as humanly possible. I cannot emphasize enough that if a woman is going to get involved in serious self-defense training (even a short class) they need to approach it realistically and become totally involved and committed to it. *Thinking that you know what you are doing or that you are proficient and not being so, can be a dangerous mistake.* We all need to know our limitations and know realistically what we are capable of.

How do you find a good instructor or self-defense guide? Like any commodity we buy we have to wade through the sales pitches, lies, cons and nonsense. We all do it everyday and it's unfortunate that getting what we are looking for is sometimes so difficult. Word of mouth from others that have been through training with someone is a great way to find an instructor or school. If you trust the person recommending a teacher, I mean if you trust hers or his realism and maturity regarding self-defense, then that's a great way to find instruction. Some other things to look at are:

- Take a good look at the instructor; if he is obviously out of shape, go elsewhere.

- Visit a class and watch the instruction. Does it look realistic? Does it look like something you can get into and be comfortable with?

- Can the instructor get his knowledge across? I had a friend that was a world-class fighter that I asked to teach some fighting moves to the students of a school I had years ago. He was terrible. He just could not interest, motivate and most importantly could not impart his knowledge to them. Not every one, even accomplished individual's can teach.

- Go and watch a class, if it's not allowed don't even consider the school.

- Consider (not mandatory) a class that has male and female students so you can practice on men, which can add to the realism.

- Look for an instructor, school or class that devotes about 90% of instruction on self-defense training.

- Take a class for a "test ride", if it's offered. Some teachers will let you take a few free classes to see if you like it.

- Stay away from schools or teachers that offer many flashy moves like high kicks, jumping kicks or so many hand strikes to a person's face that you feel that you're watching a cheap martial arts movie.

- Remember your goal is to learn to survive, keep your focus on the goal, what will work for you, discern.

Different ways to Defend Yourself

There are specialized anti-rape training classes for women in certain areas of the country that can be quite worthwhile. Some of these classes or "styles" seem to be taught by impressive teachers. Talk to the teachers and watch some classes. If theses classes look good to you, get involved.

Different styles of martial arts such as Japanese, Korean or Chinese styles, along with hybrid ones put together by knowledgeable teachers, are all valid forms of self-defense. It is not so much the style of martial art to consider but the style of the instructor. These traditional type martial arts usually take longer periods of time to develop and progress to street level proficiency. Just don't let that deter you; a good style with a good instructor can do wonders to help you survive.

Try calling your local Rape-Crisis Center or similar organization. They can be found in your local phone book and very well may be able to give you the names of some good teachers and schools.

Every realistic thing we see, learn and integrate into our "knowledge bank" is good. *However, you must be aware of your personal limitations.* I have seen overconfidence backfire on people. Confidence is great, overconfidence never is. Understand that *truth* goes hand-in-hand with real confidence.

Giving Yourself a Fighting Chance

Throughout this book I've discussed being aware, being prepared and having faith in you. Alcohol, drugs, and fatigue can alter our abilities to assess and function well. When fighting or being in a physical struggle with someone, fatigue can be a killer.

A trained fighter, as an example, does not necessarily have to be the better or stronger fighter. He can clinch, hold and back peddle until that big strong guy he is fighting gets tired. Everyone gets tired. Then, when true fatigue sets in during a fight, it can be over, no matter how talented or strong you may be. As an example, smart boxers use the tire-out strategy against stronger or more talented fighters. When fatigue sets in to the opponent, the smart fighter quite often has such an upper hand that it's sometimes essentially over right then and there. He either knocks him all around the ring or just plain knocks him out. Fatigue can end it all for you too.

At times when we are afraid, fatigue comes on quicker. When we are nervous our hearts beat faster, we breathe faster and thus we can tire quickly.

When I was younger and working out regularly, I remember being able to fight eight or nine two-minute (Karate) fights and just breeze through them. Hardly even getting tired. I remember the time I was getting ready to fight someone from out of state whom I thought was very good. I was nervous that I might not be able to win or I would fail, not being able to rise to the occasion. After I had fought him I felt as though I had fought twenty people. I was exhausted. It wasn't that he was that much better than the others I was used to fighting; he was good, but not that good, whereas he took that much out of me. My fatigue came from my nervousness.

Incidentally, the fight was ruled a tie by the judges, but I have to be honest, I knew inside that he really had won. I got what is often called a hometown decision.

In a serious life and death struggle, adrenaline may also pop in and *help you* with fatigue. Although, the effects may not last long enough. I know from street experience that if fatigue sets in, you may not be able to function well and as time goes on and you become more fatigued, you may not be able to function at all. Compound fatigue with being hit and roughed up and it can add up to a disabling fatigue. There is nothing worse than when your body can't do it, can't rise to the occasion. People can die in these times. Try to keep your cool as much as possible and if you're going to go for it, do it before tiredness starts to set in. At that point, quick, non-stop action counts, nothing else. You strike and strike and strike!

Alcohol and drugs can inhibit all of the positive types of responses we want in a life and death struggle. Not always, but often. The fact of the matter is, people on certain drugs can have greater tolerance to pain and have lack of inhibitions that can bring upon more strength. Personally, though, I would not want to be under the influence of anything except my un-influenced wits. Be cautious about too much consumption of alcohol.

Your Body's Chemical Helper

I mentioned that adrenalin may help you with fatigue and while it very well may, there are important facts to know regarding what adrenalin can do to you during times of stress or aggression. Adrenalin is a natural chemical our bodies have that is activated to help us fight or flight. It puts us in gear to be able to be sharp, quick and ready to be good at surviving danger.

An example that may show you what adrenalin can do to you is something that many people have experienced. If you've ever had a close call while driving where you almost hit a dog, cat, pedestrian or even another car and you had to swerve real quickly or slam your brakes on hard to avoid hitting it, you'll understand. Let's go on; you were able to quickly rise to the stress and missed hitting the animal, human or vehicle in the roadway. Then, immediately after you missed hitting what you so desperately strived to avoid, you start to shake, feel weak in the knees, or when you talk your voice shakes.

Sometimes, for some people it gets pretty noticeable where the person appears really scared. Well, what happens in these instances is that a major stress occurs and the body releases or dumps adrenalin to help you rise to the occasion to handle it. It's a good thing that your body does to help you react well. In this instance, you missed hitting whatever, and you were successful...but now this short-term stress is over and the adrenalin is still in your body. It ended quickly for you because you braked or swerved very rapidly and the stress lasted a second or two. Although, now the adrenalin that boosted your body is still there and is causing those totally normal physical reactions or symptoms.

When you're in a stress situation such as being attacked, adrenalin will be activated. The problem with adrenalin in these instances can be that it most likely will hamper your fine motor coordination and your cognitive reasoning, which is just to say somewhat complicated or technical self-defense moves most likely will not work for you.

The best thing to do to not be hampered by this phenomenon is to use simple basic moves, techniques, behaviors and strikes. Fancy stuff is not what you want because most likely it will not work unless, and this is a big unless…you practice these certain fancy moves, over and over, and you are experienced in the world of fighting and self-defense. *So for most of us, simple is the way to go for your survival.*

Adrenalin-dump is a serious phenomenon that many experts believe is one of the most important issues to deal with regarding women's self-defense. Adrenalin is a helper for your survival but you must know how best to exploit it. The solution is to use *simple moves* to survive…simple works.

Being Frozen in Fear

People literally have become frozen in fear when confronted by enormous stress. Or a more accurate way of putting it would be people have been frozen to non-action by being overwhelmed by shocking circumstances. As an example, men and women, when confronted in mass shooting's similar to the ones that occur every now and then in our country, have literally stopped and completely frozen-up instead of jumping on the assailant or running away when they could have. Enormous stress does not only mean shooting situations by any stretch of the means; any shockingly violent circumstance can qualify.

Were these men and women cowards or genetically inferior to the men and women that, as an example, can work through similar incidents in a war zone? No, they were not. They most likely were overwhelmed and went into a form of shock, where their minds just couldn't cope. This phenomenon can and does happen. However, listen up close…as a good military drill instructor might say, because this is the way to work through tragedy and shocking circumstances, so you DO NOT FREEZE UP.

- *Understand*—from this moment on, terrible things such as witnessing someone being stabbed, shot or being beaten badly may occur and it very well may even occur to you. Realize, know and believe that gruesome, shocking, ugly incidents can happen to you, and it may even happen today.

- Believe—that you will be able to do something by relying on your life-instinct to run, fight or to use a tool or weapon to "make it" (upcoming chapters will give you specific strategy information).

- Commit—to the fact that you will fight back no matter how bad, ugly or shocking the situation is that you're confronted with. Fighting back of course, means fighting, but it could also mean running away or as a wise man once said advancing to the rear; whatever works for you for that particular incident. Although, you will fight, no matter what. You *can* make it.

These mental conditioning steps are the foundation for beating the shock effect.

9

Defending Yourself in an Attack

In the beginning stages of writing this book, I flat out said I would not put any specific self-defense moves or techniques in it, as most books do. The reason was because I always had a great deal of difficulty in believing that picking up a book on self defense can really impart enough useable knowledge to help people. After advice from a renowned book expert on how best to help my readers, I gave the suggestion consideration. After all, my goal is to help women and the best ways I can get help across, is what I'm going to do.

I decided that I would offer some basic moves that would be simple, realistic and completely learnable from a book. Quite often books have fancy, unrealistic techniques for their readers. You won't find this here, you'll find things that you can easily understand and integrate into your life.

I know that some people learn in non-traditional venues. As an example, a very accomplished karate tournament fighter once told me that one of the toughest fighters he ever faced was a man that came off the street one night and walked into the Dojo, or karate studio where he was working out. While karate tournament fighting is not to be mistaken with street reality fighting, this particular school was known for their realism and tough fighters. Well, this young man walked into the school and asked to fight any of the teachers or accomplished students. It was pretty shocking for many of the people in the school to have someone just walk in and challenge everybody, kind of like one of those cheesy martial art movies.

Nevertheless, as I said the school was known for being realistic and tough, and one of the better fighters, if not *the* best fighter in the school, took on the challenge and the two started fighting. The fight lasted about 10 minutes and the formally trained fighter from the school got the upper hand and I guess you would say won. However, he told me it was such a tough fight for him that he had to do everything in his power to get the upper hand. They both shed blood and really got physical but he came out on top.

There's really nothing unusual about this story until you get to the point about the guy off the street who never, ever, took one formal lesson in his life! Not one. He watched movies and read books. So, he learned to be very good in an unusual, non-traditional way. The fact of the matter is that people can learn self-defense moves if presented in an easy and realistic manner.

In helping you to be the best you can be, survival wise, we'll start off with the most important elements, the basics of self-defense. Basics are the foundation for many, if not all sports. The basics of a good golf swing, as an example is a foundation that alone makes your game at least tolerable. Plus, tolerable in the self-defense "game" is surviving. So, what follows are basic, simple, workable techniques that hurt people and can stop attackers. The first three are:

- Foot stomp

- Eye gouge

- Biting

Using your Foot

The foot stomp is just that, you are going to stomp on the instep of a person's foot with your foot, or more specifically with the heel area of your foot. To get the idea in your mind, imagine wearing high heeled shoes with pointy or stiletto heels. Then lifting your foot up about 2 feet and stomping it down on a man's bare, shoeless instep, (top of his foot) with all of your might. That's the idea and goal when doing a foot stomp.

In a perfect world, you're wearing high-heeled shoes or spiked-heels, he's wearing no shoes and you're able to reach his foot and stomp down, hard. If this were the case and you stomped down on that foot, I'll guarantee, and I really never guarantee when it comes to self-defense, but I'll go out on a limb and guarantee that the man on the receiving end of that stomp would scream, moan, cry-out and stop just about whatever he was doing, at least for a short while. Just thinking about it makes me cringe...ouch! Plus, the odds are pretty good that he wouldn't be able to chase you either, right? However, this again is in the perfect world.

The odds are that he would be wearing shoes and you might be wearing sneakers. That's okay, because it can still work well. Now you have the idea of what we are trying to do when we do a foot stomp. Here are the specifics of how it's done:

When doing the stomp from the front or when facing your attacker, start by standing with your feet about shoulder width apart.

- Lift your right knee up to a horizontal position. At the same time, turn the right side of your body towards the man (now your side is facing him).

- Now, you have your leg up, horizontally, and your side is facing him. With the edge of your foot, kick it out at the area of where his knee meets his shin (general area you're aiming for).

- Continue that kick and its force down the length of his shin down to where the shin meets the foot.

- The force of the initial kick and sliding down the shin to the ultimate ending place on the foot is all done with as much force as you can gather, however, the final resting area of the stomp, his instep is where you bare down with every once of power and force you can muster.

- If it doesn't work the first time, bare down again and strike down directly on the foot, bypassing the shin as your guide. Sometimes three or four attempts are needed to damage or hurt an attacker.

What you are trying to do is hurt him and either have him let you go or stop his action against you. After doing this move it can be followed up with another technique or possibly a strike, which we will cover a little later on. The goal of course is to have him stop and this also may be a great time to run away from the attacker.

When Grabbed from Behind

Being grabbed from behind is a common way of being attacked. Some experts say that it's because predators are cowards. Well, that very well may be a reason but the fact of the matter is that it's the best place to grab anyone. It is the most effective way to control or damage someone. Using your foot though can be used here also, and here's how it's done:

- As you as you are grabbed go with the flow, that is to say that he may move you forward or backwards, go with that movement.

- While going with the general flow lift your leg at the knee and stomp down hard on his foot using his shin as your guide.

- The problem with stomping from the rear is that it's hard to know where his feet may be. When you move back following his lead, on the right foot as an example, you step roughly where he had just had his right foot. Then without having to look, you can judge where his foot is, because it will be in line with your left foot. Think about it, by following his lead you most likely will know where his left foot is. Give it some thought and understand it in your mind.

- Try to strike when you are balanced, your power will be greater.
- Use him by holding onto his hands (if he's grabbed you in a bear-hug as an example) to brace or balance yourself.
- If you have to, strike down several times.
- Even if you happen to land on his toes more than further up, keep stomping.

If he loosens up or lets go, run, get away.

You can practice the foot stomp by finding a pole or post or other similar object that can mimic an attacker's leg. Imagine the ground or floor it leads to as his foot. At first, practice the move very slowly and lightly. The key to learning many self-defense moves such as this one is slow, light, and repetitious training of the mechanics.

Do it many times, the move takes a few seconds at best, and to practice it 10 times in one session will take no time at all.

Keep your mind focused on what you are doing. You're striking the edge of your foot out to his shin (pole), sliding your foot down the shin to his foot (ground) and striking down as hard as you can with your heel. Now, you should not do it, or at least be very careful doing the move with power as this particular one can hurt your foot if it's done too hard while practicing. Proper learning of the mechanics of the move and then speeding it up to real time can make the move second nature for you.

Getting to the point of this or other self-defense moves being second nature is what you want to strive for. Second nature means that if someone attacks; you immediately go into this move, in an instant. Fast, hard and quick. After that if needed, another move can come into play, quickly, second naturedly. This continues until the attack has been stopped or you are able to get away.

Read the foot-stomp explanation and fully understand the mechanics (it can be a little difficult understanding it when reading only) and then practice it. Get it into your unconscious mind.

Using your Teeth to Get Away

Biting is not something that many self-defense teachers or schools tout. I on the other hand do, because it works if done properly. As an example a few years ago the heavyweight boxing sensation Mike Tyson was fighting a very strong, accomplished and skilled opponent, Evander Holyfield. During the fight Tyson for whatever reason broke a big boxing rule and bit a piece of Holyfield's ear off. Yes, you read right, bit a piece of his ear off.

This was on nationwide television and shocked everybody that saw it. The two men were in the middle of the ring, clinching (right on top of each other) when Tyson literally bit a piece of his ear right off. The piece fell on the ring floor. It took Tyson about a second to do it. What is interesting for us to note is what Holyfield did when it happened to him. He stopped his actions right away and turned away in pain. Who wouldn't? And that's the key, who wouldn't.

I know of another situation where two men were fighting and the bigger, tougher, more skilled fighter had the other man in a hold from which he just couldn't get away from. He bit the man in the thigh, hard, until he let go of him. The man who let him go was a strong, hardened, criminal type individual. Biting worked to get him off.

Our jaws are extremely powerful and teeth can rip flesh and break bones. Biting is close and personal and to most normal people is kind of gross thing to do. But so is being sexually molested or being raped. How do you bite?

- When in close, and an ear, nose or finger are at at-hand (or in this case at-mouth) you bite it hard, as if you were biting it off. That's right, as if you were biting it off.

- When biting, you can't bite to scare or with the intention of trying to slightly hurt. If the bite does not work it may not only enrage the attacker even more, but it most likely will alert him to be on guard for being bit again.

- So you must bite with the goal of taking his nose, finger, ear, penis or whatever area you are biting, off. Hard and with bad intensions. No hesitations.

- Very often as is with biting there may be no second chances. The first time may be the only time.

How do you practice this one? I don't know of a way to practice biting, it's a natural easy action and the hard part is mostly mental. You must have the mental attitude of being able to do it, as hard and as long as you can to stop the attacker.

Using the Eyes to Get Away

The eyes are very sensitive and as with using any force and weapons attacking eyes should be used only if need be. Some trainers will say only use the eye gouge as a last resort. Well, this book is for women to survive serious attacks. Serious attacks call for serious responses. *Force is a last resort* or more specifically put it is an option to be used only when needed. Striking the eyes can be used when you feel that you are in threat of serious physical harm or death. If it is needed for you to survive an attack use the eye gouge. Here are the basics:

- Use your index finger and your middle finger and stick them straight out. Bend the remaining fingers out of the way and use your thumb on the bent fingers to keep them out of the way. Basically you're making the peace sign.

- Spread the outstretched fingers apart, again as if you were making the sign for victory or peace. It's a very simple, natural move.

- Aim at the assailant's eyes and shoot your fingers out at both of his eyes. One of the two fingers should reach their targets.

- If you're close to hitting the eye, the natural contour of the eyes will guide your finger or fingers into the eye proper.

- Do not hesitate; strike out hard and as fast as greased lightning.

- If you miss or if need be, strike again and again and run away at the first opportunity.

See diagram #1, below, for a visual explanation:

Diagram #1

If the attacker is wearing glasses use your five fingers on either hand to simply claw or scoop them off of him in a downward motion, and then immediately use the finger gouge with either the same or other hand.

Another way to attack a predator's eye in the attempt of being successful in survival, is in using the technique I explained in Chapter 7 about the apple and the eye. That one is a very close and personal form of eye attack, but used correctly can end an attack.

You can practice the eye gouge by drawing a circle or face on a piece of paper. Draw eyes on it. Hang the paper so it flaps easily or place it in front of something soft like a pillow. Practice the gouge slowly and lightly at first and speed up to real time and real power. Do it 100 times a day. In two weeks you will be dead accurate and if you ever need to use it, it will be second nature, and I for one would not want to get in your way, you'll be that good with it. Remember, this is a good strike to run like the wind, once it's delivered well.

Strikes to Help You

There are many strikes or blows you can use against an attacker. There are punches, strikes with different areas of your hands, elbows, forearm strikes, knees, kicks and head-buts.

I've chosen to showcase just two because they are easy to learn by just reading a book and they can work without a lot of classroom training and practice.

The first one is a Hand-Heel strike or also commonly called a Palm-Heel. It's easy to make a Hand-Heel strike the way I'm going to show you because it's just about like holding your hand out as you would to wave to someone. It's really not much harder to do than the common hand wave. Look at diagram #2, below.

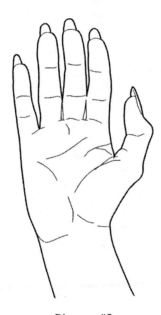

Diagram #2

Hold your left or right hand out in front of you, preferably your stronger hand. Hold all the fingers straight up as if you were telling someone to stop. Do it exactly like if a car was coming at you and you were going to put your hand out and say, stop. Now that you have your hand out, you can pull it closer to your body, about a foot or so from your chest is good. Now, spread all your fingers about a quarter of an inch apart from each other; your thumb you can spread about an inch from your hand. Now bend your wrist back towards the back...or more simply toward your shoulder, just your wrist. Do that until it gets tight and can't go back any further. Now bend your wrist forward from that point, about one inch and stop there. Tighten your hand now, your wrist included; stiffen it. Now you're ready to strike that hand out at the nose or chin of an assailant. You will strike your target with the *heel* area of the hand, see diagram #3.

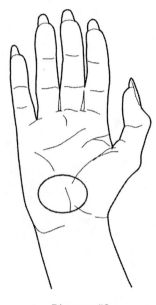

Diagram #3

You do not want to have your hand all the way back toward your forearm, like when it wouldn't go back any further because you could jam your wrist if you hit something that way. But if you are about an inch away from having it all the way back and you tighten that hand of yours it will be strong and solid and ready to hurt someone.

Explaining it another way, make a hand as you would to wave hi, to someone. Bend it back a little, making sure not to bend back too much, spread the fingers, tighten the hand and wrist and strike it out focusing with the heel or bottom of the hand…simple.

You can forego any spreading of the fingers if that is difficult for you. I find that spreading them adds to the tightening and strengthening of the hand. However, holding the fingers together is totally acceptable, but don't forget to tighten your hand and wrist right before you strike with it.

This strike is good because it's so simple to make and also to use. It's especially good to use for a strike to the nose. When you hit someone in the nose, it's pretty shocking. It makes the person getting hit, no matter who it is, close his eyes for at least a moment or two. Then the eyes start to water. When you use a hand-heel to the nose, it may very well be the time to make a run for it, away from his danger and to your escape. See diagram #4:

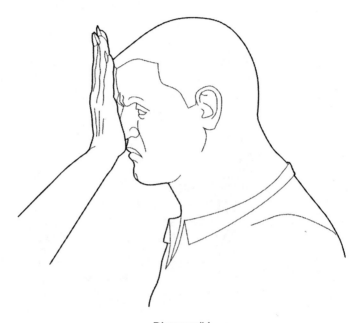

Diagram #4

The palm-heel can be practiced easily by striking at an imaginary attacker in front of you. Start slowly and lightly and strike out into the air, at the imaginary man. Speed up and give the strike full power, eventually. You can also practice this move on practice bags or specialized striking pads.

The second strike is just a punch. Use an ordinary fist or knuckle punch that's seen on movies or just about any show where there's some level of fighting. The reason it's used on every show that has fighting in it is because it works.

Basically, you're just making a fist and hitting someone with it. When I first got into different styles of martial arts that I wasn't familiar with, I remember one teacher who went on and on and then on some more, telling me about the correct way to make a fist. He would tell me to wrap my fingers a certain way, to bend my wrist just right at a certain angle, and to focus only on a certain surface of my knuckles. He got so technical with me that when he was done I had no idea on how to make a fist. Besides, I was a kid that had boxed a great deal and punched tons of practice bags way before being over-taught by this teacher, all over the same fist that some kids fighting in schoolyards just pick up naturally.

Granted, not holding your hand tight or your wrist straight can have bad consequences when you strike something, like a face or even a practice bag. Just realize, it's not rocket science and by going too far with a basic move, one can cause more harm than good.

So, to make a fist easily and one that works, start by sitting down in a chair. Imagine that there is a nail that needs to be pounded into your right or left thigh, yes you read right, a nail into your thigh. Not a good thought but don't forget we are only imagining. Imagine that the nail is sticking in your thigh and you need to pound it straight down. Now, using your stronger hand and imagining that nail is in the same thigh (right hand, right thigh) tighten the hand hard, as if you were making a tool to pound that nail down like a hammer would. Keep your wrist straight and make sure you're hand is real tight. Your knuckles are pointing away from you while the bottom of your hand is facing your thigh and the imaginary nail.

I'd bet if I were standing next to you right now, you'd have a pretty good fist made. See diagram #5, which shows how the fist looks from the front and see diagram #6, which shows how the fist looks from below (the side facing your thigh). Take a look and see if your fist looks like it should. I bet it does.

Diagram #5

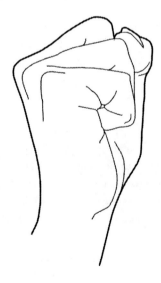

Diagram #6

If you were to strike down on your thigh that fist would be called a hammer-fist. The striking surface on your hand is the bottom (diagram #6). That hammer-fist punch can be used to strike down on an attacker just like you were imagining hitting down on your thigh. Or it can be used to hit him really anywhere you can reach him with it, as an example to the nose, see diagram #7.

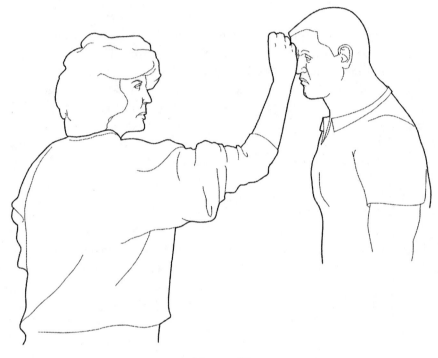

Diagram #7

If you want to use your knuckles to hit someone, more similar to what's seen on television, you hit with a different surface of the hammer-fist, the knuckles. You do not have to turn your wrist to do this. Just strike your fist forward with the knuckles going for the target instead of the bottom. With this way, your hand is in the exact position as the hammer-fist but now you are striking with the knuckles, as an example, to the nose. See diagram #8.

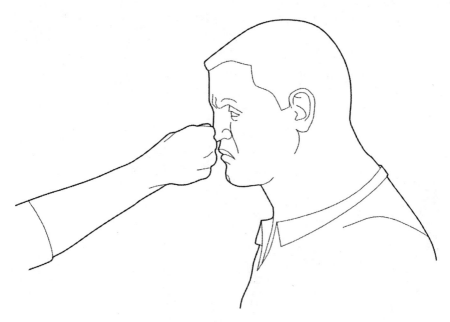

Diagram #8

Lastly, the final way to hit with a fist is the one seen most commonly on television, movies and in real fighting. Everything is the same as before; now, simply turn your fist to where your fingers are now facing the ground, your thigh or that imaginary nail, again. That's the common fist and it too can be used to strike an attacker in the nose or chin or anywhere else you can reach. The knuckles are the striking point. See diagram #9.

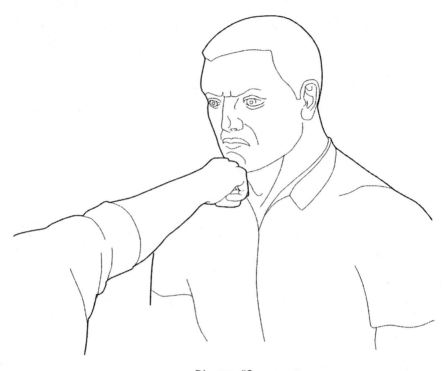

Diagram #9

These punches are best practiced on striking pads or punching bags. Striking pads are simply other striking "surfaces" that may be smaller and shaped differently than traditional punching bags. Remember to keep your fist tightly closed and your wrist tight and straight. You do not want your wrist to bend when you hit a bag with power. Keep it straight and tight.

When using punching pads or bags for practice it is *mandatory that you wear bag gloves.* These are made specifically for practice punching and will save your hands from scrapes, cuts or fabric burns that are caused by your knuckles scraping over the bags surface. They, along with punching bags can be purchased at any sporting goods store. Punching pads may be a little harder for you to find than in the average sporting goods store. You may have to special order them from a sporting goods store, the Internet or a specialized company that carries them.

There are also life-sized, rubberized punching "bags" that look and are shaped just like a man. They have a face, nose, eyes and torso. These, believe it or not can be bought at many large chain sporting goods stores. They are fantastic. They look just like a man, they can be hit hard with any kind of punch, strike or kick and you can really gauge you power, timing and accuracy when using them. The base is filled with sand or water, keeping it from falling over when you hit it. I'll say it again, they're great. It can't get more realistic when you practice your punches or strikes on this type of "bag".

10

BEING RAPED, THE AFTERMATH, and how you can survive and flourish

If you are raped or sexually assaulted, you must understand and *believe* that a woman is never, ever at fault for being raped. Never. No, really means no, nothing else. Not granting permission really means just that, not granting permission, anytime. Stop, really means stop, nothing else. It's simple. *So understand you're not at fault.* You are alive and you will mend both physically and mentally.

If you are sexually assaulted:

- Get to a safe place away from the man that violated you.

- Call a friend, relative or law enforcement personnel who can help you immediately.

- Do not remove anything from the scene of the assault.

- Do not wash your hands, brush your teeth, bathe, shower, douche or use the toilet if at all possible.

- Do not drink or eat anything or chew gum.

- Go to the nearest hospital for an examination. Ask the hospital to conduct a rape kit exam. This will help to preserve evidence if you chose to report the incident, then or later.

- If you suspect you may have been drugged, ask that a urine sample be collected.

- If you want to report the assault, notify the police immediately.

I wholeheartedly recommend any female that is sexually assaulted report it to the police, file charges and do whatever is necessary to bring the abuser to justice. However, there are women that do not want to report or file charges for sexual assault or rape. Some of the reasons for this as reported by a research report; *The Rape in America Report* are:

- 71%, listed "family knowing"
- 69%, thinking it was her fault
- 68%, people outside of the family knowing
- 50%, name being made public

Another survey from *The Violence Against Women Report* found that the primary reasons rape victims actually do not report are:

- 28%, afraid of reprisal from the offender
- 17%, police won't do anything
- 11%, police can't do anything
- 4%, Survivors feel that they will not be believed, that reporting will be futile, and they will be victimized by the system

Feelings that are Normal

After sexual assault you may experience feelings of denial, disbelief and shock. You may also have a sense of wanting to get on with your life and putting the experience in the past. This is *normal* and can last months. Feeling this way, you may just not want to get involved by reporting your incident or in pressing criminal charges.

However, as time goes by you may change your mind. You are a responsible individual and I'll not insult your ability to make sound decisions. Although, I will tell you options and possibilities which you may like to consider. If you change your mind later and wish to press charges it may be more difficult than if you would have done it right away. That's okay; you can do things at your own pace. What is important though, is that you go to a hospital straight away after your attack and get an exam for your health *and* for the collection of evidence that can be used later, if need be.

Justice; Whatever it Takes

As far as I am concerned sexual abuse cannot be tolerated and anyone committing it should get his just dues. I'm not talking about revenge, here, I'm talking about doing whatever you can to take this person off the street and get him to feel the wrath of justice. You can't take a woman and punch, kick, frighten, and sexually violate her without with out *dire* consequences.

Times are Changing for Women

Sexual assault prosecution may be difficult, but other crimes can also be difficult to successfully prosecute. I have a problem with some getting the word out that sexual assault cases can be hard to win, which in turn scares some women from going ahead *and even reporting it*. Everyday that goes by there are better advocates for women in this area (prosecutors and others), better understanding of the dynamics (research, facts accumulated) that make up sexual assault cases, which all increase the likelihood of truth prevailing for the victim. Every now and then we'll see a negative case come to the forefront, sometimes high profile ones, but sexual assault prosecution has come a long way for women.

You can increase the chances that your offender will be brought to justice by preserving the scene of the assault, preserving the evidence that may be on your body and also getting a medical examination. One could look at her body as a tool, now, that will help take the attacker to justice. Physical evidence such as seminal fluid, hair, blood types and flesh scrapings can be used as compelling evidence in your favor.

By going forward, **you** will be taking this man now…to justice. He won't like the trip, but you'll have police, prosecutors, friends, relatives and support groups behind you sending him where he belongs.

The women police officers whom usually deal with rape victims, in my experience are extremely caring and helpful. You will have an advocate in your corner. There also are support groups out there that can gather around you, help you in many ways and be an emotional safety net for you, if you ask. You do just that; ask for help, you may be surprised by how many people will help you. Average Americans are outstanding people and given the opportunity, they are unbeatable to have on your side.

11

Custom Made for Your Needs, the way YOU choose what you need to be safe

This book has gone through a lot of different things you can do to be safe. Jokingly, throughout the years I've said to friends that the perfect way to be safe, is to hire a big burly guy and put him in the middle of your living room with a big shotgun, and have him watch over you 24 hours a day, seven days a week. I guess you could also couple that with an alarm, guard dog and oh yeah, pepper spray on your waist.

However, even with all that stuff we still wouldn't be *perfectly safe*. Close maybe, but not one hundred percent. Plus, that would really be terrible to live life like that, wouldn't it?

Of course, doing all that is ridiculous and using everything mentioned in this book isn't what you should do either. If you were in a war zone or something similar you could, but for you, women who are thinking of positive, normal steps an intelligent person can pick from, *personalized possibilities abound!*

There are many things that you can pick and choose that will make sense for you and your life. Knowledge is power. The more we know about anything, the easier it is to get by or function. That's what's so good about learning—it actually makes things *easier* for us (now if we can only make kids believe it). Knowledge presented in this book is for you to look at and decipher *for your own* or possibly *your loved one's needs.* Trust yourself in using what will help you. Take it easy, be aware, be positive and above all be an optimist.

Women Sticking Together

Do not forget that you are a part of a large community of sisterhood. Help each other when you see a sister in distress. If you see a woman with a flat tire or stranded, do what you can to help her. If you see one who is getting physically abused, help her, go out on a limb, do what you have to. Take a risk, if *that's the only thing that will work.* Be a part of it all. Be supportive in any way you can. You are strong, resourceful and part of an extended family, the family of womanhood and ultimately the family of humanity.

SO in closing, above all, wherever you happen to be or whatever you happen to be doing, *slow down* and ask yourself, is there anything I need to do that will keep me safe, sound and around for tomorrow? After what you've read in this book and the thoughts it provoked in your mind; you'll find the answer.

About the Author

Steve Kovacs is a former police supervisor who has served in positions as Patrol Officer, SWAT team member, Police Supervisor, Department Training Officer and Police Regional Training Coordinator. He has been involved in the Martial Arts since the age of eight and was inducted into the World Martial Arts Hall of Fame in 1989. Steve has taught hundreds of women, men and children unarmed self-defense. He also teaches handgun fundamentals and safety for those wishing State of Ohio concealed weapon licenses. In addition, Steve has taught Private Security and Investigation at the college level and is General Manager of an Ohio based investigation and security company that services clients throughout the United States. He is a Certified Security Supervisor (CSS) and also is certified in Homeland Security (CHS). Along with his other activities, Steve also serves as Assistant Managing Director for The Jiu-Jitsu Black Belt Federation of The United States of America (JJBBF).

To contact Steve, you can e-mail him at info@securityandsafety.us

978-0-595-38208-8
0-595-38208-8

Printed in the United States
46970LVS00006BA/19

9 780595 382088